the teaching
REVOLUTION

the teaching
REVOLUTION

RTI, Technology, & Differentiation
Transform Teaching for
the 21st Century

WILLIAM N. BENDER
LAURA WALLER

CORWIN
A SAGE Company

A SAGE Company

FOR INFORMATION:

Corwin

A SAGE Company

2455 Teller Road

Thousand Oaks, California 91320

(800) 233-9936

Fax: (800) 417-2466

www.corwin.com

SAGE Ltd.

1 Oliver's Yard

55 City Road

London, EC1Y 1SP

United Kingdom

SAGE India Pvt. Ltd.

B 1/I 1 Mohan Cooperative Industrial Area

Mathura Road, New Delhi 110 044

India

SAGE Asia-Pacific Pte. Ltd.

33 Pekin Street #02-01

Far East Square

Singapore 048763

Acquisitions Editor: Jessica Allan

Associate Editor: Allison Scott

Editorial Assistant: Lisa Whitney

Production Editor: Amy Schroller

Copy Editor: Matthew Sullivan

Typesetter: Hurix Systems Pvt. Ltd.

Proofreader: Victoria Reed Castro

Indexer: Judy Hunt

Cover Designer: Scott Van Atta

Permissions Editor: Karen Ehrmann

Printed in the United States of America

Library of Congress Cataloging-in-Publication Data

Bender, William N.

The teaching revolution: RTI, technology, and differentiation transform teaching for the 21st century / William N. Bender, Laura Waller.

p. cm.

Includes bibliographical references and index.

ISBN 978-1-4129-9199-5 (pbk.)

1. Teaching—United States. 2. Educational change—United states. 3. Educational technology—United States. 4. Response to intervention (Learning disabled children) 5. Individualized instruction—United States. 6. Mixed ability grouping in education—United States. I. Waller, Laura. II. Title.

LB1025.3.B457 2011

371.1020973—dc23

2011024510

This book is printed on acid-free paper.

11 12 13 14 15 10 9 8 7 6 5 4 3 2 1

Contents

Acknowledgments

Corwin gratefully acknowledges the contributions of the following reviewers:

Judy Brunner
Author, Consultant, University Faculty
Instructional Solutions Group & Missouri State University
Springfield, MO

Laurie Emery
Principal
Old Vail Middle School
Vail, AZ

Amanda McKee
Secondary Math Teacher
Johnsonville, SC

Linda R. Vogel
Associate Professor
University of Northern Colorado
Greeley, CO

About the Authors

 **William N. Bender** is an international leader who focuses on practical instructional tactics with an emphasis on response to intervention (RTI) and differentiated instruction in general education classes across the grade levels. In particular, Dr. Bender has written more books on RTI than any other author in the world, two of which are best sellers. He has now completed seven books on various aspects of RTI, as well as a professional development videotape on that topic. He completes between forty and fifty workshops yearly in the United States, Canada, and the Caribbean. In the fall of 2010, he was selected to work with the Ministry of Education in Bermuda to establish their nationwide RTI framework. One of his recent books, *Beyond the RTI Pyramid*, was a 2010 finalist for the Distinguished Achievement Award for Excellence in Educational Publishing.

Dr. Bender uses practical strategies and easy humor to make his workshops an enjoyable experience for all, and he is frequently asked to return to the same school or district for additional workshops. He consistently receives positive reviews of his professional development workshops for educators across the grade levels. Dr. Bender believes his job is to inform educators of innovative, up-to-date tactics for the classroom, rooted in current research, in an enjoyable workshop experience. He is able to convey this information in a humorous, motivating fashion.

Dr. Bender began his education career teaching in a junior high school resource classroom, working with adolescents with behavioral disorders and learning disabilities. He earned his Ph.D. in special education from the University of North Carolina and has taught in leading universities around the nation, including Rutgers University and the University of Georgia. He is now consulting and writing full-time and has published over sixty research articles and twenty books in education.

Laura Waller is an exciting, young, dynamic educator and the co-author of *RTI and Differentiated Reading in the K–8 Classroom.* Ms. Waller began her career as a reading specialist in elementary education, working at an inner-city school in Washington, DC. With degrees from both Appalachian State University and Johns Hopkins University, she succeeded in her teaching of English-learning students, underprivileged students, Title I students, and many other students who struggled in reading and mathematics.

Ms. Waller is now teaching underprivileged children in a rural school in North Carolina and doing workshops for educators on technology for reading instruction and differentiated instruction in core academic areas. She also offers workshops on classroom use of Smart Boards, e-assessments, and other technologies to facilitate differentiation and academic progress. She recently received funding from the Bright Ideas Grant to implement hands-on literacy centers that support learning with a focus on technology and preparing students to be globally competitive in the 21st century. Her instructional practices have been featured in a professional development video, *Differentiating Math Instruction* (Corwin, 2009).

Introduction

The "Three Sisters": RTI, Technology, and Differentiation Are Changing the World of Teaching

"In a world changing drastically, what can we imagine our future to be?"

IMAGINING

The famed songwriter, and some would say philosopher, John Lennon once invited us to imagine a new world.

The civil rights leader, and many would say the stand-alone moral leader of the 20th century, Dr. Martin Luther King invited us to dream what might be, thereby providing us with a vision to guide human interaction—a vision of kindness, nonviolence, and understanding.

The great Mahatma Gandhi imagined a world in which political and economic justice would be achieved through nonviolence. He created that reality for the first time in history with the sheer power of his single-minded will.

And from a text sacred to Christians, Jews, and Moslems alike, we read, "God said, 'Let there be light!' And there was light."

These examples show the amazing power of imagination. The power of thought is fundamental to the Jewish, Christian, and Islamic traditions, in that God's imaginings—his very words—created our world and breathed life into our species. Each of the men mentioned knew and deeply understood that singular fact, as shown in the amazing power of their dreams, their imaginings. Human thought, imagining, is a profound creative power of will; it can and frequently does change the world. If the pen is indeed mightier than the sword, then the power that drives the pen—the power of the mind, the power of imagination—is the most profound power of all. Imagining is the most influential creative force in our universe.

As parents and educators concerned with our schools in the early decades of the 21st century, we might use that creative power to imagine into existence an education for our children. If our world is already in transition, as we believe it to be, then we should, we must, use our imagination to guide that transition, that teaching revolution. At the very least, these thoughts might provide us the freedom to ask some profound questions about teaching and learning in the 21st century, such as,

"How do we want our children to experience learning?"

"How are our children experiencing learning in the midst of the current digital communications revolution?"

"What can we imagine schools of the future to be?"

"What might schools become if we free ourselves from all the trappings, practices, and disappointments of today and truly imagine infinite possibilities for our students in the 21st century?"

OUR IMAGININGS

Here are a few initial thoughts—our imaginings, if you will—on education, teaching, and learning in the 21st century.

- Imagine freedom to learn any time and anywhere.
- Imagine an empowering curriculum that all students find worthy and actually want to study.
- Imagine teaching without whole-group lesson plans or unit-based instruction.
- Imagine collaborative, real-world projects as the basis for all or most of the school curriculum, thus harnessing the cognitive power of students everywhere to solve problems in society.
- Imagine all learning as project-based learning, rooted in real-world problems and engaged in a never-ending search for real-world solutions.
- Imagine the power of using student preferences, student voice, and student choice—and not textbooks or curricular standards—as our primary guide to what we teach.
- Imagine formative assessment processes designed to spot and respond to specific learning problems almost immediately, as students experience them.
- Imagine using technology as the primary engine for, and basis of, the freedom to learn.
- Imagine teachers as supportive facilitators of learning, not as class leaders or group policemen.
- Imagine a teaching/learning process that is immediately responsive to the academic and behavioral needs of every individual student.

- Imagine a wired digital classroom; smartphones, or laptops on every child's desk, as well as one at home, used constantly by students to engage in high-quality learning activities.
- Imagine immediate and complete interconnectivity in the digital world, controlled and mediated by the mind, not a keyboard.
- Imagine the Internet, organized appropriately to serve as both the curriculum and the assessments for our students.
- Imagine students educated to use such a learning system, carefully separating the gems from the meaningless fluff—the wheat from the chaff—along the information superhighway.
- Imagine students taught in such a way that they consider learning fun.
- Imagine students receiving exactly the instruction they need, given their learning approaches and preferences, not merely instruction delivered to whole groups of students who happen to be the same age.
- Imagine a curriculum wholly created in the 21st century, for the 21st century.
- Imagine a world where "political correctness" or any other attempt to limit thought (e.g., burn books, identify or limit hate speech) is viewed as a distorted misunderstanding. In that imagined world, all ideas are free to stand or fall on their own merits.
- Imagine students who are able to tell the difference between fact and opinion, or between informational stories and today's "media opinion" shows or comedy shows that masquerade as news.
- Imagine all assessment as dynamic, authentic assessment rooted in projects that lead to creative answers for real problems in society. Why should we waste the profound collective energy of learning by millions of students on "made up" problems? Can't we learn to let students work and solve real problems?

Given this rather broad list of imaginings, we can make a few initial observations. First, these are merely the rambling thoughts of two educators who have collectively participated for many decades in the educational system and have, for years, reflectively questioned that system. We freely acknowledge that other educators, while perhaps sharing some of these thoughts, would certainly have other imaginings; of course, we cannot know what those might be. Given that rather profound limitation, we do invite them to communicate directly with us or others about these thoughts and ideas. In fact, we would love nothing better than for this book to start a dialogue of imaginings on what schools need to be. Let the creative dialogue begin!

Next, in looking over the imaginings, we observe that some of these are now underway, while others seem merely distant dreams. Several of these ideas represent factors that are already at work in the marketplace (i.e., social-networking interconnectivity, or a computer on every desk, at least in some schools) and only remain unrealized in all of our classrooms because of limited budgets and, perhaps, a lack of imagination in our politicians—perhaps (dare we say it?) even in our educators.

Next, we put these imaginings down with no distinct priority but rather as a catalyst for our own thoughts. In fact, some of these seem to be directly contradictory to others. For example, how can topical studies be driven exclusively by student preference or choice? Perhaps this might lead to seeking one or more guiding principles that might govern these imaginings. If so, then what should be the driving force or guiding principles in seeking to conceptualize and perhaps enact this list of imaginings? Should there even be such guiding principles?

THE TEACHING REVOLUTION

We cannot now see the ultimate value of these imaginings, and we know not what power they may have. While some may see that as "overhyped," we believe these imaginings are quite justified, given the transformation of instruction that has, in some locales, already begun, as well as the fundamental communications changes in our digital world that are impacting and will continue to impact teaching in a profound way. In short, a drastic change is coming in the very structure of our teaching/learning process that is likely to dramatically alter the very look and feel of our classrooms and ultimately of our entire educational system. Many have already commented on this imminent change (East, 2006; Kay, 2010; Partnership for 21st Century Skills, 2009a; Tomlinson, 2010; Wilmarth, 2010). The coming changes in instruction are so profound that many of today's teachers, students, and parents might not recognize the learning environments only a decade from now.

> *Profound change is coming in the structure of our teaching/learning experiences that is likely to dramatically alter the very look and feel of our classrooms and ultimately of our educational system.*

As one example, the Partnership for 21st Century Skills, an advocacy group promoting modernization and full implementation of technology in every aspect of our schools, has recently encouraged a refocusing of our educational institutions to adequately address skills for the next century. Such content as technology skills, use of the new "mobility technologies," digital media skills, content creation, and interpretation skills, along with many other informational skills that will be critical in the digital world of tomorrow, must be more heavily emphasized in our classrooms today (see www.p21.org).

However, this group advocates more than merely adding these skills to our curriculum; rather, the very structure of knowledge is likely to change as production of new knowledge becomes based on social networking and actual creation of knowledge by students, as opposed to using these new technologies merely to make information available to students (Kay, 2010; Wilmarth, 2010). When that transition takes place—a transition that many see as imminent—our current instructional practices will seem as dated as required courses in blacksmithing. In 2010, as this book was in preparation, an emphasis on these skills did not characterize most classrooms (Kay, 2010). However, the change is coming (Partnership for 21st Century Skills, 2007, 2009a, 2009b), a fundamental transformation of education, involving everything from the design of our schools to the constant use of technology, into something that more closely resembles the productive environments that now characterize our businesses in the modern world.

More so than technology, however, other changes are dramatically restructuring our classrooms. Response to intervention (RTI) is another change in instructional procedure that is currently impacting our students and will soon impact all teachers across the grade levels (Bender, 2009a; East, 2006). The importance of this instructional paradigm has grown far beyond its roots in special education eligibility discussions, and the impact of RTI in classrooms today cannot be overemphasized. Elementary classrooms around the nation are functioning very differently today than did the same classrooms in 2005 or 2007, as a result of the implementation of RTI (Bender, 2009a). As this book goes to press, middle and high schools are exploring the same profound change.

Finally, the concept of instructional differentiation (Tomlinson, 1999, 2010), an idea that has guided our instructional endeavors for a decade, has now matured, leaving its roots in multiple intelligences theory far behind and transforming into a new instructional model for classrooms at all grade levels (Bender & Waller, 2011; Tomlinson, 2010; Tomlinson & McTighe, 2006). Because of the nationwide implementation of differentiated instruction, whole-class instruction, that icon of teaching for nearly fifty years, is likely to either significantly decrease or simply come to an end across the grade levels (Bender & Waller, 2011). It will be replaced, in large measure, by differentiated instruction framed in learning centers or by using other differentiated instructional models such as project-based learning, creation of knowledge through social-network-based digital environments, or cooperative instructional practices. Perhaps most instruction will ultimately be computer or web based, facilitated but not led by the teacher. Such instruction promises to be not only effective but also much more individualistic. Student voice and student choice will play a much larger role in what is studied and learned.

Of course, today's digital communications media, by and large, did not exist when Tomlinson published her initial work on differentiation in 1999, and that demands the following question: What opportunities do modern digital and social-networking media such as *MySpace, Facebook,* or *Twitter* hold for differentiated instruction? As this book was written (late 2010 through February 2011), the whole world witnessed a never-before-seen lesson on the impact of online social networking. An actual revolution, the "Twitter Revolution," took place in the streets in Egypt in February of 2011, leading to the downfall of the head of the government, largely resulting from the amazing power of digital communications media—communications media that only seven years ago did not exist.

The sheer power of the social-networking, digital media phenomenon has surprised nearly everyone, and given technology today, it is hard to imagine where differentiated instruction—coupled with these technology-based digital tools, computerized learning environments, or totally individualized, web-based curricula—can ultimately lead. Most proponents of technology describe these developments as an extremely fast train, increasing in speed exponentially and heading into what is now termed the *singularity*. The singularity is defined as the moment when technological change becomes so rapid and so profound that it causes a fundamental rupture in the fabric of human history (Grossman, 2011). At the singularity, technology embedded within artificial intelligence, coupled with today's automated manufacturing power, makes human beings both unnecessary and, some might say, obsolete.

The singularity might also be seen as the moment in time when artificial intelligence overtakes and surpasses the brainpower of all human beings worldwide, and the growth curve in a variety of technological fields suggests this may happen sometime between 2020 and 2045 (Grossman, 2011). Some scientists are seriously discussing the migration of the human mind into software at the point of what, in the 20th and early 21st centuries, was called *death*. Those scientists predict virtual immortality as individual human beings outlive their bodies and continue to live and thrive in the form of complex software programs. Others who study the singularity suggest that combinations of nanotechnology and bioengineering may preclude human "death" entirely, making these speculations about "human personality" software moot. Further, data from those fields, once again, suggest a technology growth curve and time frame for reaching the singularity in 2045 (Grossman, 2011). These discussions, from serious scientists, remind one of the computer known as *Hal* in the famed movie *2001: A Space Odyssey* (1968) overtaking human decision making and ultimately controlling human destiny—a *Hal* on steroids, if you will! As educators, we must ask, what does the teaching/learning process look like as we approach the singularity? With nanotechnology leading to computers much smaller than the eye can see, and those computers eventually embedded literally within the human brain, our Internet and social-networking interface will be both seamless and instantaneous at the singularity. What does learning look like in that world, when all access to all digitally recorded human knowledge is immediately accessible to everyone?

Lest anyone suggest that the singularity is pure science fiction, we should point out that the singularity was originally identified at a NASA symposium as early as 1993, and today, the Singularity University, with a very impressive faculty, offers a series of graduate study programs for a highly selective group of future leaders (Grossman, 2011). The university's summer program in 2011 will be hosted at the NASA Ames Research Park, in the heart of Silicon Valley. In short, these are highly talented, highly skilled scientists and leaders in the technology industries holding serious discussions on the future of technology and humanity.

Again, what does this mean in classrooms next year or the year after, or perhaps five years from now? How will teaching and learning be transformed within the next two, five, or ten years? Educators must consider these drastic technology changes—and perhaps even this approach to singularity—and what they might mean for the classrooms of this and the next decade. If we do not undertake these discussions now, we risk becoming increasingly irrelevant in the world of today's "wired" generation. While there is little consensus on the singularity, and even less agreement on the other rather dramatic, futuristic propositions, there is one point that all advocates of technology in the classroom do agree on: Our current instructional procedures are clearly and woefully inadequate in preparing our students for the 21st century (Dretzin, 2011; Kay, 2010; Partnership for 21st Century Skills, 2009a, 2009b; Wilmarth, 2010). We must, as responsible educators, ask, "In order to do our best for our students, where do we go from here?"

In this book, we have chosen to consider most of the possibilities—the imaginings already mentioned—within an overall educational structure that is rooted in these three dynamic changes in education: the infusion of modern technology into our classes, RTI, and differentiated instruction. We believe that fundamental transition in both our society and our classrooms is already underway as a result of these changes, and we have chosen to structure this book based on these factors. Initially, three innovations in instruction—the three sisters—will be described as the basis for the coming dramatic change in the teaching/learning process. While RTI and increased use of technology are relatively recent changes, the shift to highly differentiated instruction, we believe, provides a fertile basis for the other two. Each of these, by itself, represents a rather profound change in the dynamics of the classroom, and the combined impact is likely to be a *dynamic synthesis* of innovation that is transitional in nature, providing a second-order change in instructional technique within the classrooms of the future.

Three innovations in instruction—the three sisters—provide the basis for the coming dynamic change: RTI, communications technologies, and the shift to highly differentiated instruction.

However, this coming revolution is an example in which *the whole is greater than the sum of the parts.* The synthesis is dynamic in that the symbiosis of these rather dramatic changes extends and multiplies their overall individual impact in such a way that these innovations will soon create a catalyst for dramatic reformation in teaching. Thus, we believe, as do many others, that a revolution in our teaching/learning structures is coming and that some of the imaginings may come to fruition sooner rather than later.

In developing various books over the last decade, we became cognizant of a "dynamic" shift that is currently underway—a critical mass for change in our teaching/learning structures—which we believe is founded, primarily, in these three areas. Our effort here is not intended to provide an extensive premier of these changes in teaching and learning but rather to introduce each of these briefly in an effort to show how these innovations are dramatically, and collectively, impacting classrooms today.

After describing the "imaginings" wrought by these changes—changes that are already underway—we will go further, speculating on how these changes may drive education over the next decades. We hold absolutely nothing sacred in our current educational practices—to do so would be a disservice to our imaginings. But we will track our discussion logically with guidelines and suggestions for using the emerging communications technologies based on what innovative educators are already doing, as well as current curricula standards, innovation in brain-compatible instructional practices, the nature and context of meaningful change in education, and the fundamental question of what is important to learn in and for a 21st-century world.

At the very least, this promises to be an exciting, if not profound, intellectual endeavor, and we invite our readers to come along. Let the journey begin!

> *We hold absolutely nothing sacred in our current educational practices—to do so would be a disservice to our imaginings.*

1

Beyond Response to Intervention

Teaching as It Ought to Be!

The emerging response to intervention (RTI) initiative may best be understood, in broad terms, as a commitment among educators to *change a child's life.*

That is, RTI is intended to change students' trajectory of learning or behavior from a growth curve that leads to failure to a growth curve that leads to success for struggling students (Bender, 2009a). For advanced students, RTI represents a commitment to challenge them to the very limits of their abilities and skills, and then beyond. To create such profound change, RTI includes a commitment to provide whatever educational and behavioral interventions might be necessary, at whatever level of intensity, to create that positive change in students' future. As authors in this area, we realized that this definition is somewhat different from other definitions of RTI that have been proposed, but we are confident that this definition places the emphasis exactly where it should be: on the individual student. Thus, the best understanding of RTI is that this instructional approach is intended to change a child's life.

In fact, evidence has shown that RTI has already drastically transformed reading instruction in the elementary grades and has begun to revolutionize education across all grade levels and content areas (Geisick, Graving-Reyes, & DeRuvo, 2008; Gibbs, 2009; James, 2010; Legere & Conca, 2010; East, 2006; Protheroe, 2010; Rozalski, 2010; Stewart, Benner, Martella, & Martella, 2007). Perhaps more than any other single factor, the RTI initiative is leading the revolution in instructional strategies. Here's an example: As recently as 2007, most elementary teachers were not conducting a reading screening for every student in the class three or more times a year, nor were intensive systematic interventions routinely provided for struggling students. Today, nearly all elementary teachers are conducting such universal screening as well as providing highly structured interventions under the RTI initiative (Bender & Larkin, 2009). Thus, when students display significant delay in developing early reading skills, rigorous interventions with small groups of students are taking place to ameliorate those delays. This represents a major restructuring of educational practice (East, 2006).

> *The recent RTI initiative has restructured elementary reading and has begun to restructure middle and high school instruction as well.*

Today, virtually every state is currently implementing RTI in reading in the primary and elementary grades, and many middle and high schools are currently developing RTI models for the upper grades (Duffy, 2007; Gibbs, 2009). In that sense, schools are much more responsive today to students' learning needs in reading than ever before, and this represents the actualization of one of the imaginings presented in the introduction to this book. For reading in the elementary grades, at least, we may have already attained the lofty goal of identifying and then meeting every student's instructional needs.

Initially, most schools implement RTI in reading and mathematics, but many schools are likewise implementing RTI procedures to alleviate behavior problems in the classroom as well (Stewart et al., 2007). Thus, teachers even in those higher grades will soon be participating in RTI in one or more of these areas, if they are not already doing so (Duffy, 2007; Fuchs, Fuchs, & Stecker, 2010; Hoover, Baca, Wexler-Love, & Saenz, 2008; James, 2010; Protheroe, 2010).

Of course, reading has been an educational priority, and the vast majority of states began their RTI efforts in the area of elementary reading (Bender & Larkin, 2009). Today, the strongest research base for RTI is in that area (Berkeley, Bender, Peaster, & Saunders, 2009; Fuchs & Deshler, 2007; Fuchs & Fuchs, 2007; Legere & Conca, 2010). However, as early as 2005, educators around the nation began to turn their attention to applications of RTI in other subjects such as mathematics (Bender & Crane, 2010) or in other grade levels such as middle and high school grades (Duffy, 2007; Gibbs, 2009; Johnson & Smith, 2008; Rozalski, 2010). In short, RTI is likely to impact how nearly every teacher in the public school age range conducts his or her class, and as such, this may very well be the single most important innovation in education in decades (Bender, 2009).

EXACTLY WHAT IS RTI?

Realizing that some readers may not be completely familiar with RTI, it is probably wise to begin with the basics. As noted previously, we see RTI as an effort to improve a student's trajectory of learning or behavior. However, a more conventional definition will help one understand the profound impact RTI is likely to have in education. Most definitions of RTI suggest that the RTI process may be defined as a set of systematic, increasingly intensive educational interventions that are designed to target an individual student's specific learning challenges (either academic or behavioral) and to provide a supplementary intervention within the context of the general education class—that is, aimed directly at those learning challenges to assist the student in progressing through school (Bender, 2009; Boyer, 2008; Fuchs et al., 2010; Hoover & Love, 2011).

> *RTI may be defined as a set of systematic, increasingly intensive educational interventions that are designed to target an individual student's specific learning challenges and to provide a supplementary intervention within the context of the general education class.*

Using RTI, it should be possible to assist virtually every struggling student during the critical early grades and hopefully to prevent significant problems later in school. Based on changes in federal legislation in December 2004, the federal government now allows the RTI procedure to be implemented as one component of the eligibility determination for students suspected of having a learning disability (Bradley, Danielson, & Doolittle, 2007; Fuchs et al., 2010; East, 2006). However, in the larger nationwide RTI efforts, a student's eligibility for learning-disability services is a secondary issue (East, 2006). RTI has emerged from its early roots in special education and is now, first and foremost, a fundamental restructuring of instructional options and interventions within the general education class, focused on assisting all struggling students. Under an RTI framework, if a teacher sees a problem in the basic skills of reading, mathematics, or behavior, that teacher is both committed and obligated to provide an intensive, research-based intervention that is designed to alleviate that problem (Bender, 2009). Further, almost all of the RTI process take place in those classes well before eligibility for special education is considered (Fuchs et al., 2010; Hoover & Love, 2011; East, 2006), indicating again that eligibility for special education is a secondary concern in RTI.

The "Revised" RTI Pyramid of Intervention

RTI is typically described in terms of a pyramid of interventions, such as that presented in Figure 1.1, and while many educators are now familiar

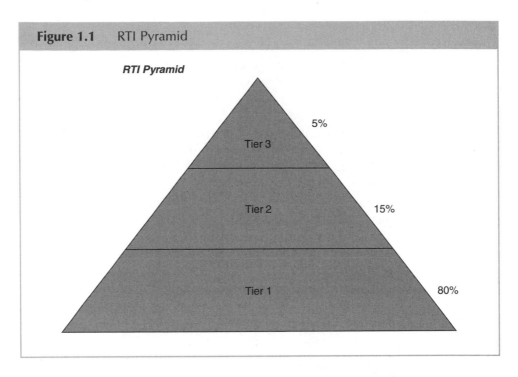

Figure 1.1   RTI Pyramid

with this pyramid, those experienced in RTI realize that this overall model must now be modified or revised somewhat to present an accurate picture of how RTI is currently implemented in schools. In this section, we have described the original RTI pyramid, as well as the essential modifications of the original concept, to show both those changes in the RTI model and how the RTI initiative is transforming classrooms across the nation (Bender, 2009).

The pyramid of intervention is usually divided into three or more instructional intervention levels, or *tiers*, and each tier represents a different level of intensive intervention designed to alleviate the learning problem (Bender & Shores, 2007; Fuchs et al., 2010; Hoover & Love, 2011; Kame'enui, 2007; Protheroe, 2010). By 2009, approximately 73 percent of the states had adopted a three-tier pyramid model for their RTI efforts (Berkeley et al., 2009; Spectrum K–12, 2009), similar to that pictured in Figure 1.1.

In this model, Tier 1 was originally described as instruction provided for all students in the general education classes (Bender & Shores, 2007; Fuchs et al., 2010; Gibbs, 2009). As the model suggests, every student experiences instruction at the Tier 1 level, which is why this tier is presented as the largest in the model. However, as the percentages within the original three-tier model indicate, this level of instruction is typically described as meeting the educational needs of perhaps 80 percent of the students in the class (Boyer, 2008; Bradley et al., 2007; Fuchs & Deshler, 2007), while the remaining 20 percent of the class is described as needing more intensive instruction to meet their educational goals.

While initial discussions of RTI around the nation took those percentages as "holy writ" (Bender & Shores, 2007; Boyer, 2008; Bradley et al., 2007; Fuchs & Deshler, 2007), more recent descriptions of RTI have raised questions about those percentages, leading to some revisions in the RTI model (Bender, 2009; Bender & Crane, 2010). In fact, those percentage estimates are based on reading instruction in the elementary grades, specifically from research on primary reading in programs such as *Reading First*, and thus these general percentages are probably inaccurate in other subjects such as mathematics or in the higher grade levels (Bender, 2009; Bender & Crane, 2010). As one example, reading deficits may compound over time, resulting in increased reading deficits in the higher grade levels. Therefore, as many as 30 percent or 35 percent of the students in middle and high school grades may not have their instructional needs met for reading in Tier 1 instruction during the high school years (Gibbs, 2009). This suggests that a higher percentage of middle and high school students might need to progress to the more intensive tiers of instruction within the RTI model.

> *Over time, reading deficits may compound and result in increasing deficits demonstrated by more students in the higher grade levels; thus, the percentages presented in the original RTI pyramid might be underestimates.*

At the Tier 1 level, the general education teacher provides all of the instruction (Bender & Shores, 2007). Thus, general education teachers are expected to deliver instruction for large and small groups, as well as some individual assistance based on the individual needs of the students. Further, as described in the literature on RTI (Bender & Shores, 2007; Boyer, 2008; Bradley et al., 2007; Fuchs & Deshler, 2007; Fuchs et al., 2010; Kame'neui, 2007), primary and elementary teachers also have the responsibility of conducting individual screening assessments for all students to identify students who are struggling. The term *universal screening* is used among proponents of RTI to represent the fact that these screening assessments are undertaken for all students in the class, and such screening is usually conducted three times each year. Data from those universal screening assessments are then used to identify students who may need more intensive instruction at the Tier 2 level (Fuchs & Deshler, 2007; Fuchs et al., 2010).

> *Universal screening measures are screening assessments in basic skills that are undertaken for all students in the class and are typically conducted a minimum of three times each year.*

While this model works fairly well in elementary reading and mathematics, it is not clear from the research literature how universal screening might be implemented in middle and high schools (Duffy, 2007; Johnson & Smith, 2008). In fact, there is virtually no research literature on either screening procedures or general RTI implementation for high schools or middle schools (Johnson & Smith, 2008). Therefore, this question of who is responsible for universal screening assessments at the Tier 1 level, like many other questions, is still an open question for the higher grade levels (Deshler, 2010; Gibbs, 2009). Again, this universal screening might require some revision of the initial pyramid of intervention, in terms of the duties of general education teachers in the upper grade levels.

Tier 2 interventions include supplemental, targeted intervention for a small group of students who are struggling academically in the general education class (Boyer, 2008; Fuchs & Fuchs, 2007). Again, this general percentage may not be accurate in all subjects or in the higher grade levels (Gibbs, 2009). However, using this figure as a basis, in a typical class of twenty-four fourth-grade students, one might expect that between four and six students would be struggling in their reading and that they would thus require a supplemental, Tier 2 intervention.

> *Tier 2 interventions include supplemental, targeted intervention for a small group of students who are struggling academically in the general education class.*

The good news is that Tier 2 interventions work for the majority of students, as shown by rather extensive research in the elementary years; in fact, as many as 85 percent of students, or perhaps even 95 percent, typically have their needs met through a combination of Tier 1 and Tier 2 instruction (Bender, 2009a; Bender & Larkin, 2009). Again, educators should exercise caution in extrapolating those figures to RTI interventions in subjects other than elementary reading as well as in the higher grades. Like the Tier 1 intervention, the general education teacher is expected to deliver this Tier 2 level of targeted, intensive instruction for those struggling students (Fuchs & Fuchs, 2007), at least in the lower grade levels. It is not yet clear if this expectation is appropriate for middle and high schools.

Tier 3 is described in the literature as a very intensive, highly specific instructional intervention (Fuchs & Fuchs, 2007; Johnson & Smith, 2008). Of course, such intensive instructional interventions take considerable teacher time, and that has become a concern during RTI implementation. Further, in some school districts or states, this level of instruction takes place after a child is identified as needing special education services (Fuchs et al., 2010; Fuchs & Fuchs, 2007; Johnson & Smith, 2008). However, in other states, the Tier 3 intervention is required prior to any eligibility decision (Kame'enui, 2007; East, 2006). Therefore, educators are urged to check the eligibility regulations in their own states and school districts to determine when students may participate in Tier 3 interventions.

Because of these issues, there is considerable disagreement in the literature on RTI concerning who is responsible for Tier 3 instruction. While many RTI proponents agree that Tier 3 should be a function of general education, in most cases reported in the literature, there is virtually no example in which general education teachers were responsible for the actual daily delivery of Tier 3 instruction (Bender, 2009a; Duffy, 2007; Fuchs et al., 2010; Gibbs, 2009; Johnson & Smith, 2008), even though some state plans indicate that general education teachers are responsible for such instruction. Rather, other general educators (e.g., math tutors, reading coaches, or intervention teachers) conduct almost all of the Tier 3 interventions described in the current literature (Bender, 2009a; Fuchs et al., 2010; Gibbs, 2009; Hoover & Patton, 2008; Johnson & Smith, 2008).

The Tier 3 level of intensive intervention is frequently described as one-to-one instruction and is designed to meet the needs of the remaining 5 percent of students with intensive instructional needs (Fuchs et al., 2010; Fuchs & Fuchs, 2007). Given a class size of twenty-four students, one might expect that only one or two students may require this level of intensive intervention, and research has shown that many of those students will respond positively to highly intensive instruction (Fuchs & Fuchs, 2007).

Finally, students whose needs are not met by intensive Tier 3 instruction are typically referred for consideration for special education services. As this indicates, most RTI efforts take place prior to eligibility considerations, and in that example, data generated from these RTI procedures may be used to help determine the eligibility of some students for special education programs (Bender, 2009a; Fuchs & Fuchs, 2007).

As can be seen in the preceding discussion, there are many open questions about the applicability of the initial three-tier pyramid RTI model. Nevertheless, this model provides the basis for most state models of RTI, and as such, this broad model will be used in this book. Throughout this discussion, we will show caveats, modifications, or questions about the applicability of this model. However, regardless of these recent concerns and questions, educators should make no mistake: the three-tier pyramid of intervention is one of the most influential instructional innovations in recent decades, and this model will drastically refocus how almost all teachers conduct their classes within the next decade.

> *The three-tier RTI pyramid is one of the most influential changes in education in decades, and this model of instruction will drastically refocus how almost all teachers conduct their classes within the next decade.*

Common RTI Elements

As stated already, virtually every state has now adopted or recommended some type of RTI model, and some states have described the tiers in various ways that differ from the preceding general description (Berkeley et al., 2009; Hoover et al., 2008; Hoover & Love, 2011). However, in spite of these state-to-state differences, there are a number of common elements to most if not all RTI models (Bender, 2009a; Bender & Shores, 2007; Kame'enui, 2007). These are presented in Box 1.1.

Box 1.1   **Common Elements in Most RTI Models**

- Emphasis on universal screening three times each year in Tier 1
- Emphasis on a set of increasingly intensive interventions, structured into intervention levels that are referred to as *tiers*
- Emphasis on the use of research-based curriculum in each tier
- Frequent progress monitoring of each individual's performance in each tier
- Data-based decision making
- Team-driven determinations on students' placement in the RTI tiers

---

First, all RTI models include some emphasis on universal screening to identify students struggling in various subjects. Most states have focused on reading initially, though RTI procedures to assist students in mathematics and improving behavior are also common (Bender, 2009a; Bender & Crane, 2010). Universal screening in any of these areas is typically the responsibility of the general education teacher, and most states now require such universal screening in reading at least three times each year in the primary and elementary grades.

Next, all of the RTI models present some concept of increasingly intensive education interventions that are, as indicated, referred to as *intervention tiers* (Bender & Shores, 2007; Kame'enui, 2007). In the literature, it is clear that proponents of RTI assume that students will progress through these tiers in numeric order, such that struggling students are placed in Tier 2 interventions prior to Tier 3 interventions, and so on (Bender & Shores, 2007; Berkeley et al., 2009; Hoover et al., 2008; Kame'enui, 2007).

Next, all RTI models require the use of a research-based curriculum as the basis for instruction provided within the various intervention tiers. Further, frequent progress monitoring of each student's performance in each tier is also required to document the efficacy of the intervention for each student (Kame'enui, 2007). Again, this aspect of RTI implementation represents the actualization of one of the imaginings in the Introduction. This performance monitoring becomes critically important should students not have their needs met in the various tiers and subsequently be considered for special education. Finally, data-based decision making by a collaborative team should be used to interpret the child's progress relative to curricular standards (Bender & Shores, 2007; Kame'enui, 2007).

A CASE STUDY: HELPING ALFONSO IN MATHEMATICS

The following case study of an RTI procedure for an individual student helps demonstrate how the RTI initiative is not only making a big difference for individual students but also restructuring instructional procedures throughout the school in rather profound ways. This example describes RTI in elementary mathematics. In this case study, Alfonso is a fourth-grade student who is struggling in mathematics, a subject in which he was performing well below grade level. His parents move frequently, and both Spanish and English is used in the home. Because he rarely remained in a single school for an entire year, he had never been placed in special education. Box 1.2 presents the multistep RTI process as well as the necessary documentation for this RTI procedure.

Box 1.2   An RTI Procedure for Alfonso

Pupil Name: Alfonso Gomez Age: 10 Date: 9/14/2011
Teacher: Ms. Carol Antoine School: Tidioute Charter School—Grade 4

Statement of Academic/Behavioral Problem:

Alfonso is from a home in which both Spanish and English are used, but Spanish is the primary language. He is a good student who has some difficulty in reading, but his primary problems seem to be in mathematics. He doesn't seem to know the lower times tables, and doesn't know some of the higher times tables at all. These times tables are introduced in Grade 2, and most students master the times tables by the middle of Grade 3. That is why it concerns me that Alfonso has not learned the times tables. This delay leads to problems in almost every other aspect of math. His testing scores (from another state) for the last year indicated a grade equivalent of 2.8 in mathematics. He will need an intensive intervention, initially aimed at mastering these math facts.

(Continued)

(Box 1.2 Continued)

I have shared a written synopsis of these concerns and the intervention plan below with our mathematics coach for the fourth grade, Ms. Amy Wise.

Signature: *Ms. Carol Antoine*   Date: *9/14/2011*

Tier 2 Intervention Plan

As a Tier 2 intervention, I will provide Alfonso with supplemental instruction on multiplication math facts, while stressing the concept that multiplication is merely repeated addition of the same value. I will work with Alfonso and five other students that need help with multiplication math facts three times each week for at least twenty minutes each time, using mathematics exercises from the textbook. During that time, my teaching assistant will supervise the class in a small-group science project. For progress-monitoring purposes, I will use a set of timed math facts problems that focus on automaticity in times tables. At the end of each instructional period, I will chart the number of times tables facts from the fours, sixes, sevens, eights, and nines tables that Alfonso completes correctly in one minute. We will skip the fives times tables, as Alfonso knows that set of math facts. The data completed on each Friday will be charted to monitor Alfonso's progress during this intervention. We plan to begin the intervention on next Monday, 9/18/11, and continue it throughout the next six-week grading period. I've sent a letter to Alfonso's parents informing them of this intervention.

Signature: *Ms. Carol Antoine*   Date: *9/14/2011*

Observation of Student in Tier 2 Intervention

I observed Alfonso in his Tier 2 math intervention on the times tables. Ms. Antoine used several practice worksheets from our state curriculum, as well as a math facts callout activity. She then completed a one-minute timing worksheet that included the fours, sixes, and sevens times tables (she has not yet begun work on the eights and nines times tables with this group). Alfonso completed nineteen problems correctly.

Signature: *Amy Wise, Math Coach*   Date: *10/12/11*

Tier 2 Intervention Summary

During this six-week intervention, Alfonso mastered the fours times tables but continued to have difficulty on the higher times tables. He was making little progress, and his weekly assessment data (presented in Figure 1.2) show that he will need more intensive instruction in mathematics. On

11/15/08, Ms. Wise and Ms. Lockhardt, two members of our student-support team, and I discussed these data and concluded that this intervention for Alfonso had not worked well enough to allow Alfonso begin to catch up in mathematics. Then we discussed a Tier 3 intervention.

Signature: *Ms. Antoine*   Date: *10/30/11*

Tier 3 Intervention Plan

Because I serve as the mathematics instructional coach for the middle grades at Tidioute School, I usually do most of the Tier 3 interventions in mathematics. In my math lab, I have several computers and computer-based instructional programs in math that we use for Tier 3 interventions.

We decided that an intensive intervention of thirty minutes daily was needed for Alfonso, which focused initially on multiplication tables and higher-level multiplication operations (e.g., two- and three-digit multiplication). Our software allows us to target specific skills of this nature. Therefore, Alfonso will receive his Tier 1 math instruction in Ms. Antoine's class daily, and in the afternoon he will come to the math lab for thirty minutes of intensive software-based instruction on the specific skills he needs. We will then reconsider Alfonso's further needs for math assistance.

Signature: *Ms. Amy Wise, Math Coach*   Date: *11/2/2011*

Tier 3 Intervention Summary

The student-support team reviewed Alfonso's performance in his Tier 3 intervention (see Figure 1.3) and concluded that Alfonso is making good progress in mathematics. However, he has not yet mastered all of the times tables and thus is not yet at grade level. The team recommends continuation of his work in the instructional lab for another grading period, and the team will review his progress then.

Signature: *Ms. Amy Wise, Mathematics Coach*   Date: *12/14/2011*

Statement of the Skill Deficit

This RTI case study follows a general format developed by Bender and Shores (2007) and includes the necessary documentation, summary of screening data, precise descriptions of interventions, and other essential components of the RTI process. As the summary in the first section of this form indicates, Ms. Antoine, the fourth-grade teacher, describes the specific problems demonstrated by Alfonso and relates those to his overall mathematics achievement. Ms. Antoine indicates that a skill deficit on the higher times tables is likely to negatively impact Alfonso's progress during Grade 4, and thus there is a need for this supplemental, Tier 2 intervention.

At the outset, it seemed clear that Ms. Antoine believed that some supplemental instruction would greatly assist Alfonso, since she did not note any other extreme difficulties in his mathematics work. Of course, research on RTI procedures in mathematics documents the overall efficacy of Tier 2 interventions (Ardoin, Witt, Connell, & Koenig, 2005; Bryant et al., 2008; Fuchs, Fuchs, & Hollenbeck, 2007), so Ms. Antoine had every reason to anticipate success based on the planned Tier 2 intervention. Many times, students need only a bit of supplemental assistance to master new or different subject matter in either reading or mathematics, and a supplemental Tier 2 intervention for several weeks may be all that is required.

The Tier 2 Intervention Plan

This type of highly specific plan for a targeted intervention for Alfonso represents one change that resulted from RTI implementation. When RTI is implemented, targeted, intensive interventions are provided for all students who need them, as was the case in this example. This represents one distinct change that occurs when RTI becomes the instructional model within a school, and this type of systematic, targeted-intervention support was not occurring only a few years ago in any subject area (Bender, 2009a).

This is not to say that teachers were not assisting students less formally, perhaps by additional tutoring on particular topics; effective teachers have always provided such assistance. However, under an RTI framework, this type of assistance tends to be much more structured, and many more of the resources of the school are marshaled to provide Tier 2 and Tier 3 intervention assistance as needed. Thus, these RTI interventions are much more intensive and are typically provided over a longer term for struggling students.

In this example, the Tier 2 intervention planned by Ms. Antoine is aimed directly at mastering multiplication math facts, the exact difficulty noted in the problem statement found in Box 1.2. Further, a great deal of detail is provided in this intervention plan to document what the exact intervention is, how frequently it will take place, and how the instruction time will be used. This documents the intensity of the supplemental instructional intervention at the Tier 2 level.

In Box 1.2, we should note that Ms. Antoine informed both the parents and the mathematics coach at Tidioute Charter School of her planned Tier 2 intervention. Such notification, while not required by most state regulations, is typically encouraged by local schools and school districts, and we certainly encourage a free flow of information on Tier 2 and Tier 3 interventions to the parents. Note also that in this example, Ms. Wise, the mathematics coach, actually observed Ms. Antoine delivering the Tier 2 intervention to Alfonso and the other members of her small group. Ms. Wise noted that Ms. Antoine followed the prescribed lesson plan and also noticed that Alfonso was experiencing some success. Thus, that observation served both as initial documentation of RTI and as a check on overall instructional fidelity; in short, that observation showed that Ms. Antoine was teaching this skill in an effective manner, using a research-proven instructional procedure.

Data-Driven Decision Making in RTI

The RTI process is a data-driven one that allows teachers to make meaningful and practical decisions based on a student's actual performance (Bender & Crane, 2010). Charted data that show how a student responds to instruction is mandated by the RTI process, and in this instance, the progress monitoring data from the Tier 2 intervention demonstrated that Alfonso was progressing in learning the times tables, but was progressing quite slowly.

In this example, the data chart (see Figure 1.2) and the written summary of the Tier 2 intervention presented in Box 1.2 indicated that the Tier 2 intervention worked only to a degree. It is often the case that the intervention data will show some increase, but that the increase in performance may not

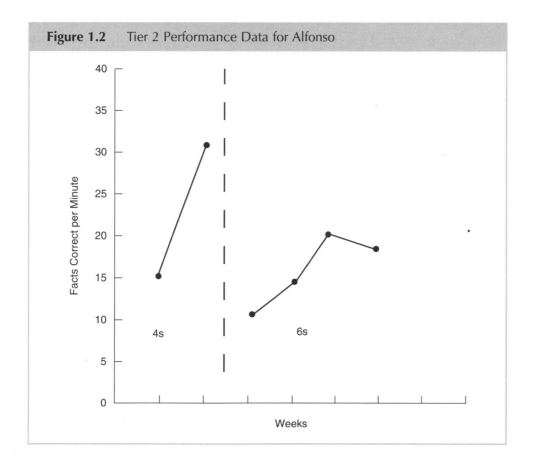

Figure 1.2   Tier 2 Performance Data for Alfonso

be significant enough to help a student like Alfonso catch up with his peers. In such a case, a Tier 3 intervention might be necessary, as it was here.

The Tier 3 Intervention Plan

As discussed previously, Tier 3 interventions are almost always conducted by someone other than the general education teacher (Bender, 2009a). In this case, Ms. Wise, the mathematics coach, delivered the Tier 3 intervention, so she developed the Tier 3 intervention plan presented in Box 1.2. Note once again that the intervention plan is highly specific and detailed. Also, the intensity of the intervention increased as Alfonso moved upward from Tier 2 to Tier 3. For example, the Tier 2 intervention involved Alfonso working in a small group with a four-to-one pupil/teacher ratio. That intervention was conducted for twenty minutes, three days per week. In contrast, the Tier 3 intervention involved individualized computer-based work targeted exactly to Alfonso's needs and was delivered daily for thirty minutes. Clearly, the Tier 3 intervention was much more intensive than the Tier 2 intervention.

Tier 3 Results

The results of this Tier 3 intervention are presented in the data chart in Figure 1.3. Like the Tier 2 data, these data indicated that Alfonso was learning his times tables but again was learning them very slowly. Still, his pace of progress did speed up considerably, and based on those data, the decision was made to continue this level of intensive intervention for Alfonso through the next grading period, or until he masters the times tables.

Next, the student-support committee noted that the data from these two interventions indicated that Alfonso was progressing. In this case, it is clear that Alfonso was responding to appropriate, intensive instruction, and thus under the new definitions, he would not be considered a student with a learning disability. In fact, nearly 90 percent of students exposed to Tier 2 and Tier 3 interventions are assisted by those interventions (Bender, 2009a); thus, RTI is significantly improving our educational endeavors for those students.

> *Nearly 90 percent of students exposed to Tier 2 and Tier 3 interventions are assisted by those interventions; thus, RTI is significantly improving our educational endeavors for those students.*

Finally, in this example, a computer-based instructional program was used, which has become quite common in our experience. Even in poorly funded schools, various computer applications are typically involved in RTI, often for documentation of efficacy of interventions (e.g., use of AIMSWeb software, as discussed later in the book), if not for actual delivery of targeted instructional interventions as was the case here. This is one area of cross-fertilization of RTI and technology, and because this is so

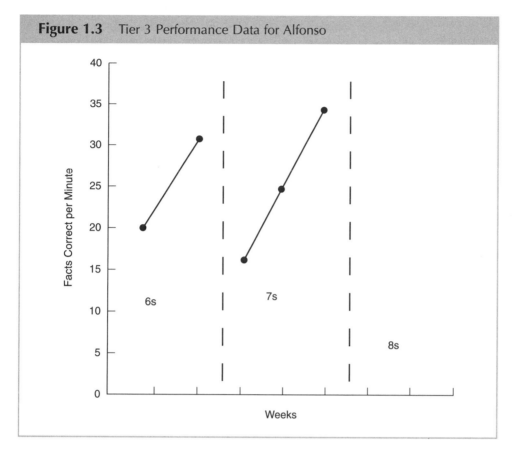

Figure 1.3 Tier 3 Performance Data for Alfonso

common, it makes little sense to us to discuss RTI without some mention of the various technology applications that facilitate it. At various points in this book, we will suggest technology applications that are in frequent use around the nation.

CHANGE THAT MAKES A DIFFERENCE!

Teacher Advocacy for RTI

As the case study makes clear, RTI involves a considerable amount of work, and after full RTI implementation in reading, mathematics, and behavior, teachers will be devoting substantial time to assisting struggling students. This represents a significant change in how classrooms operate, and such change will not come easily. In fact, school reform efforts over the years have shown that unless teachers buy in to the change process, in this case, the new emphasis on RTI, then significant improvements in instruction are neither possible nor likely (Duffy, 2007; Gibbs, 2009; Orosco & Klingner, 2010). In particular, all members of the leadership team or the professional learning community at the school should serve as advocates of RTI for RTI to be a meaningful and substantive reform effort.

Specifically, advocates of RTI must be prepared to address the question, "Why should we do RTI?"

Fortunately, the answer to that question is both simple and direct: RTI works! RTI has been proven by research to be one of the most effective instructional options available today for struggling learners (Fuchs & Fuchs, 2007; Gibbs, 2009; Johnson & Smith, 2008; Katz, Stone, Carlisle, Corey, & Zeng, 2008; Legere & Conca, 2010; Stewart et al., 2007). The caveats of this research are summarized here so that all educators can have immediate access to this information on the effectiveness of RTI; these data provide a compelling rational and justification for RTI implementation and should be shared broadly with all educators.

> *RTI has been proven by research to be one of the most effective instructional options available today.*

Further, in our experience conducting hundreds of workshops with teachers across the country on RTI, we have realized that some teachers are initially quite nervous about this innovation in teaching. When teachers initially hear of their increased responsibilities as RTI is implemented (e.g., universal screening, conducting Tier 2 interventions, etc.), they are sometimes reluctant to jump into the RTI instructional approach. However, we can also state that once teachers experience the success that RTI brings for their students, they become "sold" on the RTI model. This section presents some of the research supportive of RTI, and this is presented for one simple reason: to allow all educators to become advocates of RTI as one of the most important teaching innovations in recent decades (Fuchs & Fuchs, 2007; Gibbs, 2009; Johnson & Smith, 2008; Stewart et al., 2007).

> *All educators are encouraged to become advocates of RTI, one of the most important teaching innovations in recent decades!*

RTI Works With Struggling Learners!

First, and most important, research has consistently shown that RTI works for students who are struggling in basic skills such as reading and mathematics, including many students who are already placed in special education (Duffy, 2007; Legere & Conca, 2010; Lolich et al., 2010; Stewart et al., 2007). RTI procedures were initially implemented in the primary and elementary grades in reading, and extensive research in that area has shown that RTI is extremely effective in curbing early reading problems and in helping students get back on track toward reading success (Hoover et al., 2008; Katz et al., 2008; Legere & Conca, 2010; Mahdavi & Beebe-Frankenberger, 2009; Stewart et al., 2007; Vaughn et al., 2009). Further, early research on the efficacy of RTI in middle and high schools suggests similar success in the upper grade levels (Deshler, 2010; Gibbs, 2009; Johnson & Smith, 2008; Rozalski, 2010). Nationwide, educators have embraced the RTI initiative because research has shown that RTI works for almost all students struggling in reading. Thus, RTI represents not only the most recent innovation in education but perhaps also the very best way to teach!

> *RTI represents not only the most recent innovation in education but perhaps also the very best way to teach!*

However, more recent research has provided even more justification for implementing RTI. For example, research has consistently shown that when students are struggling in reading, the provision of intensive supplemental instruction for relatively brief periods of time can alleviate the reading problems and put students back on track toward long-term reading success (Denton, Fletcher, Anthony, & Francis, 2006; Lolich et al., 2010; Simmons et al., 2008). In some cases, computer-based Tier 2 or Tier 3 interventions presenting only a six- or eight-week intervention have resulted in reading gains of one, two, or even three years (Bender & Waller, 2011). Thus, a little intervention effort seems to go a long way in decreasing long-standing academic problems.

> *A little intervention within the intensively focused RTI model seems to go a long way in decreasing long-standing academic problems.*

While results vary significantly, the broad body of available research from primary and elementary grades suggests that between 40 percent and 60 percent of students who are struggling in reading or mathematics will have those academic problems alleviated or eliminated by a Tier 2, intensive, supplemental reading intervention (Hughes & Dexter, 2008; Simmons et al., 2008; Stewart et al., 2007; Torgesen, 2007). Further, additional research has demonstrated that many students who do not respond positively to a Tier 2 intervention will respond positively to a more intensive Tier 3 intervention (Rozalski, 2010; Vaughn et al., 2009). Taken together, the available research suggests that provision of multiple tiers of interventions in an RTI process seems to alleviate reading problems for something like 75 percent to 90 percent of the students who initially struggle in reading (Hughes & Dexter, 2008; Torgesen, 2007). Thus, RTI represents an option that could drastically reduce school failures over the years.

> *Research suggests that provision of multiple tiers of interventions in an RTI process seems to alleviate reading problems for 75 percent to 90 percent of the students who initially struggle in reading.*

RTI Reduces Disproportionality

Disproportionality is a term used to describe a disproportionately high number of African American children placed in special education classes (Artiles, Kozelski, Trent, Osher, & Ortiz, 2010; Bender & Shores, 2007).

The concern over disproportionality has been a recurring one, and no instructional idea or innovation seemed to address this problem. However, recent research on the impact of RTI suggests that it might alleviate the problem of disproportionality (Abernathy, 2008; Donovan & Cross, 2002; Duffy, 2007; Hosp, 2010).

In a pilot study from New Hanover County, NC, Abernathy (2008) reported that prior to RTI implementation, African American students were 1.7 times as likely to be placed in special education classes. However, after RTI was implemented, that ratio was reduced to 1:1 in only one year. Other similar reports have been presented recently showing the same general result: RTI seems to reduce disproportionality (Donovan & Cross, 2002; Duffy, 2007; Hosp, 2010). While these reports do not represent controlled scientific experiments, this is nevertheless an important finding. This RTI model may help solve an ongoing problem that previously seemed unsolvable.

RTI Helps Schools Meet Statewide Assessment Goals

Some schools in the nation have struggled to make adequate progress toward meeting their annual goals, goals that are typically stated in terms of meeting or exceeding state standards in reading, mathematics, and other subjects (Bender, 2009a). However, research has shown that RTI is highly effective in assisting several groups of students who typically have difficulty meeting these goals. For example, research has demonstrated the efficacy of RTI procedures for students who traditionally struggle in reading, such as students with disabilities or students who are English learners (Denton et al., 2006; Linan-Thompson, Vaughn, Prater, & Cirino, 2006; Lolich et al., 2010; Lovett et al., 2008; Rinaldi & Samson, 2008; Simmons et al., 2008), and these are the very subgroups that, in some cases, fail to meet the state assessment standards. For example, at one RTI pilot school in Montana, only 49 percent of students were meeting yearly assessment goals in 2006 prior to the implementation of RTI. After only two years of RTI implementation, however, 76 percent of the children were meeting their assessment benchmarks for reading (Mahdavi & Beebe-Frankenberger, 2009). Therefore, if schools wish to have all of their students meet and exceed assessment standards, those schools should rigorously implement RTI in each of basic skill areas.

> *If schools wish to have all of their students meet and exceed assessment standards, those schools should rigorously implement RTI in each of the basic skill areas.*

RTI Empowers Teachers

Many teachers feel empowered when they implement the RTI process (Bender & Crane, 2010; Lolich et al., 2010) because they see the academic success that RTI brings for struggling students. In RTI, teachers implement instruction for exactly the difficulty that is slowing students down, and this results in teachers feeling empowered: They sense they are making more of a difference in the lives of their students (Lolich et al., 2010).

For those of us who have taught, this sense of empowerment is completely understandable. Virtually every veteran of the classroom has felt, at one time or another, a desire for just a bit more time to help a struggling student, and implementation of RTI provides exactly that. RTI is a mechanism for providing sustained, systematic, and intensive help for struggling students in their exact area of difficulty. Further, additional resources can sometimes be marshaled to assist with Tier 2 and Tier 3 interventions so that all students receive the instructional assistance they need (Bender, 2009a; Duffy, 2007; Gibbs, 2009).

Using RTI Research as an Advocacy Tool

RTI benefits not only targeted students but also whole schools in their improvement efforts (Bender & Crane, 2010; Stewart et al., 2007). To create meaningful change in education, the school faculty must be made aware of the advantages of the change, and nowhere is that more important than in the implementation of RTI. Research results, such as those reported here, should be shared quite broadly among teachers and parents to solicit active participation in the RTI process. Implementation of RTI is typically a multiyear endeavor; some proponents suggest a three- to five-year time frame for complete RTI implementation (Bender, 2009a; Duffy, 2007), and certainly mistakes will be made during that extended implementation process. However, these research results provide a strong basis of advocacy for RTI, and these data should motivate educators to spend the time to implement this innovation across the grade levels.

HOW DOES RTI IMPACT SCHOOLS?

With these research conclusions in mind, educators must next consider how implementation of these newly developed RTI procedures is likely to change our current instructional practices. If this RTI initiative, coupled with differentiated instruction and modern teaching technologies, is to revolutionize education, it behooves us to consider exactly what that revolution might entail. As shown already, full implementation of RTI in reading, in mathematics, and for behavioral problems will drastically impact how many teachers teach, and listing the changes in instruction in a school that fully implements RTI for reading, mathematics, and behavior across the grade levels pointedly shows these changes. Those are presented in Box 1.3.

> *Full implementation of RTI in reading, in mathematics, and for behavioral problems will drastically impact how many teachers teach.*

Box 1.3   How RTI Changes Instruction

Typical Instruction Practices in 2005	School Operating Under Full RTI Implementation Today
Only state assessments were used by most teachers.	Teachers conduct universal screening three times per year in reading, math, and behavior.
Teachers assisted students with individual or small-group work as time allows.	Targeted interventions are planned and delivered to address every student's deficits.
Teachers providing assistance to student did so on their own time in general education.	Resources of the entire school are marshaled to make Tier 2 and Tier 3 interventions available.
Teachers assessed students in need less.	Progress monitoring is undertaken for all Tier 2 and Tier 3 students.
Teachers frequently made instructional decisions alone based on data from classwork and error analysis.	Data-based instructional decisions are made by a team of educators based on actual data on a student's performance on repeated measures over time.
Teachers addressed student need individually or with school-based assistance teams.	Students' academic and behavioral needs are addressed more systematically, and this improves student performance more quickly.

One rather dramatic change resulting from RTI implementation is the fact that many primary and elementary teachers are now conducting universal screening three times each year in reading and mathematics. In the future, it seems reasonable to expect that such universal screening might be implemented in reading, mathematics, behavior, and possibly writing across the grade levels, which would clearly be a major shift in emphasis in educational assessment. Previously, most educators relied on statewide or district assessment data—data that might have been one to three years old—to identify students with serious deficits. The use of more frequent universal screening procedures prevents some students from slipping through the cracks. In short, today's universal screening procedures identify problems much more quickly, and this represents a change from previous practice.

Another positive change resulting from RTI is the provision of targeted interventions that are planned and delivered much more frequently once a school has implemented RTI (Bender, 2009a). While teachers have, for many years, assisted students with individual or small-group tutorial assistance directed at certain topics, RTI implementation means that such assistance is likely to be much more systematic and intensive than it was previously. One of the imaginings presented earlier dealt with assessment practices that were highly sensitive to student needs, and we are moving toward that goal with the RTI initiative.

During RTI implementation, school faculty frequently reconfigure available resources to make certain that all students receive Tier 2 and Tier 3 interventions as needed (Bender, 2009a). In that sense, RTI represents the marshaling and possible redistribution of all the resources of the school to provide immediate help for students who need it, and this process frequently results in significant changes in overall instructional procedure. Resources can be marshaled and redistributed in a wide variety of ways to make RTI happen. In different situations around the country, teachers have found their instructional responsibilities modified to include Tier 2 and Tier 3 interventions (Hoover & Patton, 2008), or paraprofessionals are reassigned to assist the general education teacher find the time for Tier 2 instruction with a small group of struggling students (Bender, 2009a). In fact, schools have been amazingly creative in redistribution of existing resources to make RTI happen for those students who need supplemental instruction. This is a rather dramatic change in educational procedures, and faculty today are highly involved in those decisions in the schools that are currently implementing RTI.

The emphasis on data-based decision making has grown over the last two decades, and while that emphasis was not directly linked to the RTI initiative initially, it has certainly become a main focus of RTI efforts across the states. It is not an overstatement to suggest that RTI was founded on collaborative, team-driven, data-based decisions concerning each student's educational needs, and in that sense, every teacher in the building (not only department chairpersons, team leaders, or administrators) is emphasizing data-based decision making. Further, in Tier 2 and Tier 3 interventions, an individual child's progress is monitored weekly or every other week (Bender, 2009a), making this instructional approach highly sensitive to the student's ongoing education needs. Data-based decision making is at the very core of the RTI efforts.

Finally, as the research data clearly show, RTI is working to improve students' academic and behavioral performance (Fuchs & Fuchs, 2007; Johnson & Smith, 2008; Katz et al., 2008; Legere & Conca, 2010; Stewart et al., 2007). Even for groups of students who have consistently underperformed, RTI seems to make a positive and impressive difference, as shown by the research reported previously for students with special needs and for English learners.

For these reasons, it is safe to say that RTI has transformed education; RTI has resulted in the teaching of reading in a more highly responsive fashion in nearly every primary and elementary class in the nation, and again, the research shows that this works. To paraphrase a recent presidential candidate, this is change we can believe in! Further, the more the nation's educators focus on RTI, the more significant and impactful this instructional change seems to become. As stated by the National Association of State Directors of Special Education (East, 2006), RTI represents a profound change in how general educational classes operate.

> *RTI has transformed education; it has moved far beyond an eligibility documentation procedure and has resulted in the teaching of reading in a more targeted, highly responsive fashion in nearly every primary and elementary student in the nation.*

CONCLUSIONS

As shown repeatedly in this chapter, the RTI process alone promises to restructure instructional practices in elementary, middle, and high school classrooms in a profound manner (Johnson & Smith, 2008; Lolich et al., 2010; Rozalski, 2010). Educators can be confident that instruction in all classrooms either has changed or will be changing substantially over the next few years, based on RTI implementation (Bender, 2009a).

We believe that it is prudent to consider RTI in the context of the other emerging changes in education, including an increased emphasis on technology and increasing differentiation in the classroom. Again, we believe that these "three sisters of change" will reformulate instructional practices in ways never before envisioned, and the impact of these factors is presented in the next two chapters. Also, Chapter 5 in this text provides several planning procedures and suggestions for school faculties to consider in preparing to implement these changes.

2 Technology

*The Engine of Change in
21st-Century Teaching*

THE ENGINE OF REVOLUTION IN TEACHING

Independent of the instructional revolution resulting from widespread RTI implementation in our classrooms, educators around the nation have come to the conclusion that the ongoing revolution in mobile communications technologies such as smartphones and iPads, coupled with today's classroom instructional tools and the constantly developing computer-based instructional curricula, are already causing a major change in teaching (Bender & Waller, 2011; Ferriter & Garry, 2010; Kay, 2010; Wilmarth, 2010). To make this point more personal, imagine an excellent teacher, a veteran of ten years in the classroom who, for family reasons, left the classroom only five years ago and now wants to get back into teaching. That teacher probably used some software for instruction five years ago, but he or she may have left prior to installation of whiteboards in the class and therefore may not be familiar with presentation software as a teaching tool. Likewise, that teacher would probably not be familiar with e-assessments or web-based instructional programs. Of course, the use of recently developed tools and ideas—such as Twitter, e-assessments, Facebook, smartphones, or iPads—for instruction would be completely alien to that teacher.

> *The ongoing revolution in mobile communications technologies such as smartphones and iPads, coupled with today's classroom instructional tools and the constantly developing computer-based instructional curricula, is causing a revolution in teaching!*

MOBILE TECHNOLOGIES DRAMATICALLY IMPACT OUR WORLD

Mobile communications technologies are drastically changing our world, and when these technologies are coupled with 21st-century computer-based instructional curricula, they will drastically change our classrooms (Kay, 2010; Wilmarth, 2010), and that change is likely to come within the next five years. Modern technologies provide instructional and connectivity options today that were unrealized even as recently as 2008. Major shifts in instruction are predicted for the immediate future (Dretzin, 2011; Ferriter & Garry, 2010; Wilmarth, 2010). For example, on April 20, 2010, the CNN Morning News did a story on teen texting and reported the following:

Texting has increased by 600 percent from 2008 to 2010.

On average, teens text 3,000 times per month.

Some schools are struggling with the problem of texting in class.

Texting may be addictive, as increased dopamine (a neurotransmitter associated with the pleasure center in the brain) appears to be highly stimulated when teens receive a text).

Some schools are embracing smartphones as instructional tools, rather than restricting their use!

Some educators suggest that texting and the general digital connectedness of today's student is a problem for schools; however, as the last point indicates, some schools are using this very digital media to join in students' worlds, and make the curriculum more interesting to 21st-century students (Rapp, 2009). As one personal example, on April 14, 2010, the senior author of this volume was conducting a workshop at a high school in suburban Atlanta and found several teachers who had set up Facebook pages specifically dedicated to their instruction, and students were encouraged to use Facebook to communicate with them throughout the instructional unit, particularly on evenings prior to class exams. One teacher stated that, on each evening prior to a unit text, she announced that she would be available on Facebook for two or three hours to answer students' questions about the test content. She reported that she typically stayed busy connecting with her students during that entire time, as well as on at least one evening every week for two hours.

Rather than punish students for using smartphones in class, Dixon High School, in rural North Carolina, is one of a number of pilot schools that have used grant monies to provide smartphones for students to facilitate communication with teachers on difficult concepts that the students might encounter during homework (Davis, 2010a). Alternatively, those students are invited to submit questions to the "class blog" to seek answers to their questions when they are working at home.

Finally, Strange (2010) reported on a major effort to provide educational content in history and geography directly for smartphones via the Internet. In that example, students looking at a historic location would be able not only to download information from Google maps of that location but also to overlay that map with historical photos to show what the site resembled at the time the historical event occurred. As all of these examples show, the educational power of the new communications technologies and social-networking sites is nearly unlimited (Kay, 2010; Wilmarth, 2010).

It is not an overstatement to say that today's mobile devices such as smartphones, BlackBerrys, or iPads are creating a revolution in communications that, when coupled with modern educational software and classroom-based technologies, will ultimately lead to a revolution in education (Ash, 2010; Busch, 2010; Cote, 2007; Dretzin, 2011; Ferriter & Garry, 2010; Mann, Skakeshaft, Becker, & Kottkamp, 1998; McCoy, 1996; Partnership for 21st Century Skills, 2007, 2009a; Wilmarth, 2010; Wood, Mackiewicz, Norman, & Cooke, 2007). These technologies, as they are applied in various classrooms, will greatly enhance every teacher's opportunity to communicate with students, and schools may choose to either participate in this connection revolution or attempt to ignore it.

In addition to modern mobile communication options, we believe that the wide array of available, research-proven, software-based curricula can help to individualize lessons in a way not possible previously. Further, use of these technologies should characterize every classroom during the next decade of the 21st century (Cote, 2007; McCoy, 1996; Salend, 2009; Wood et al., 2007). The newly developed technology options available to teachers are nearly endless, and these provide nearly unlimited opportunities to learn. Further, 21st-century students will be using these technologies to impact their world, and educators would be remiss not to provide some guidance on how these tools may be used appropriately. Today's students will use these tools completely without adult supervision, unless both parents and school faculty begin to participate in earnest in these endeavors.

Further, modern technologies can and should be seamlessly integrated into virtually every subject area in the schools to prepare students for the environment they will face over the next decades (Ash, 2010; Elder-Hinshaw, Manset-Williamson, Nelson, & Dunn, 2006; Ferriter & Garry, 2010). In today's media-rich, high-technology world, effective teachers simply must embrace these instructional innovations to reach students (Cote, 2007; Dretzin, 2011; Kay, 2010; Partnership for 21st Century Skills, 2007, 2009a, 2009b; Salend, 2009; Wilmarth, 2010). Because most students have fairly extensive experience with various technologies in nonschool settings, schools must adapt by implementing instruction using these modern technologies as much as possible to hold the interests of today's preteen and adolescent. With the implementation of these new technologies, effective instruction in the next decade will look drastically different from instruction only five years ago (Dretzin, 2011; Ferriter & Garry, 2010; Kay, 2010; Wilmarth, 2010), and all teachers would be well advised to be prepared for these coming changes.

> *Teachers simply must embrace these instructional innovations to reach students, and effective instruction in the next decade will look drastically different from instruction only ten years ago.*

The purpose of this chapter is to present an array of these modern instructional options to demonstrate the coming changes in instruction these options entail. We do not intend this chapter to be an exhaustive catalogue of the new mobility devices, of instructional software, or of classroom instructional technologies. Due to the ever-evolving nature of these technologies, it is impossible to catalog all of the available tools teachers can use. However, the technology tools and resources listed here provide excellent starting points for teachers and administrators who are interested in providing the benefit of 21st-century learning to their students.

For organizational purposes, the majority of technology available to teachers fit into one of three basic categories: technologies that help teachers teach content in new collaborative ways, technologies that help teachers grade and evaluate their students, and technologies that allow teachers and students to build a community through the publication of information (Richardson, 2010). Again, one may well anticipate that these new and ever-evolving teaching tools will dramatically change education within the next two to five years, and that this impact will be intertwined with the RTI initiative and increased differentiation of educational activities within the classroom.

EMERGING TECHNOLOGY TOOLS FOR TEACHING

Tools that allow teachers and students to share content in new and innovative ways provide an entirely new mechanism for learning, and most important, many students today are excited by innovative use of these new technologies in schools! In particular, tools that allow for sharing of content free the instructional process from the old methods of textbooks and encyclopedias, and open new worlds of exciting information for teachers and students. To prepare students for the world of the 21st century, teachers must explore and employ these new technologies for informational sharing in the instructional process.

> *To prepare students for the world of the 21st century, teachers must explore and employ these new technologies for informational sharing in the instructional process.*

Google Docs

Google Docs (docs.google.com) is a free word processing resource for sharing, creating, and editing documents online that supports Word documents, spreadsheets, and PowerPoints. To use Google Docs, teachers and students must create a free Google account, and once that is done, sharing and collaborating on documents is fairly easy. The teacher (or student) creates a new document, saves it, and then sends the document to other users for them to view or for their collaboration. Any of the invited users can edit the document at any time. All of the revisions are archived, and any of the previous revisions can be undone. This makes group work that much easier for teachers and students.

There are several ways to use Google Docs in the classroom. A fourth-grade teacher may have small groups of students working on a research paper about North Carolina history, as one example. One student could be researching the flag, another the state motto, and another the Tar Heel legend. Once a document is created and uploaded into Google Docs, students in the group can add in their sections, review other sections, and offer constructive feedback. Students can contribute to, edit, and comment on the document as long as they have access to the Internet. The file does not have to be e-mailed from one computer to the next when changes are made; in Google Docs, the changes appear on the document for the entire group to see. If the changes are not acceptable, the students can revert back to the previous form of the document—all revisions can easily be undone. When the group is done, the teacher can use Google Docs to make comments within the students' writing. This allows for immediate feedback for students.

In one sense, this type of interactive assignments represents a fundamental change in the traditional teaching/learning process. By having a technology platform that allows students to work together so intimately, and review and critique each other's contributions as they are done, the student group itself becomes a *formative evaluation* process even as the students continue the task. Students will be constantly checking and correcting each other's work, even prior to the teacher realizing that such small-group corrections are taking place. In short, students can essentially create knowledge with and for each other, and this represents a substantive change from the traditional, teacher or textbook (or video) delivery of knowledge that characterized traditional classrooms (Ferriter & Garry, 2010; Wilmarth, 2010). This collaborative, self-correcting creation of knowledge process represents a fundamental change in learning, and many students find this much more interesting and exciting than the traditional types of classroom assignments because of the "connectedness" with other students (Wilmarth, 2010).

Google Docs can also help teachers go paperless in the 21st-century classroom. Using this tool, teachers can create forms for a variety of learning activities, and once a form is created, teachers can embed that form onto their class wiki. Students and parents can access the wiki, fill out the form, click submit, and the answers are immediately sent back to the teacher. This is a great way to do a quick pop quiz or fill out a student information sheet.

Edmodo

Edmodo (www.edmodo.com) is a free resource that provides opportunity for sharing classroom content in a Twitter-type fashion. Students and teachers are able to share links and files, post assignments, create class calendars, and create and respond to posts. To use Edmodo, teachers create a free account and then invite their students to join. Students then sign up using a teacher-generated code.

Once the page is created, teachers can send and post messages to the entire class, small groups, or individual students. Students can also respond to posts in this format. However, those student responses can only be directed to the teacher or to the class, and this prohibits private, student-to-student communications, for safety reasons. Still, using this tool, teachers can post assignments or alerts about upcoming due dates, and can even take student polls on various aspects of issues within the lesson. Teachers can also upload files to the class library and check to see when students have turned in assignments.

To assure ease of use, Edmodo is compatible with mobile phones and allows teachers and students to communicate at any time using mobile technology. This effectively extends the school day in a way that is comfortable for both students and teachers. Students and teachers can opt to have alerts sent to them via text messages, tweets, or e-mail.

Using Edmodo, students are likely to be actively engaged with the content and connected with class expectations. For example, a fifth-grade science teacher must cover using technology to build understanding of weather and climate, and students must be able to decipher the various types of clouds and their relation to the weather patterns. Using the Edmodo platform, the fifth-grade teacher can upload a poll question asking students to correctly identify the type of cloud present around their neighborhood as they arrive home from school. Students can answer the poll and then post comments about the type of cloud in their neighborhood and the weather pattern that is accompanying it. In this manner, Edmodo encourages continual engagement with scientific content, vocabulary, and applicable technology. Further, because this platform is so similar to other communication activities that students enjoy doing (i.e., texting, Twittering, etc.), there is likely to be high participation, even from students who would not normally complete their class assignments (Wilmarth, 2010).

TeacherTube

Like the ever-popular YouTube, TeacherTube (www.teachertube .com) is a video-sharing website designed for teachers. Teachers and their students can create content, perhaps an edited presentation about their hometown, and then post that knowledge to the world in this venue. Although the primary use is educational videos, TeacherTube also presents photos, documents, and audio selections for teacher use. Students in many classrooms have already uploaded their own videos—videos created as an assignment and based on their course content. Teachers can find videos on anything from state capitals (http://www.teachertube.com/viewVideo .php?video_id=15395&title=50_States_and_Capitals__cartoon_song_) to teacher-made raps about calculating perimeter (http://www.teachertube .com/viewVideo.php?video_id=157&title=Mrs__Burk_Perimeter_Rap).

TeacherTube serves as a free resource that has the potential to truly motivate students. Using a brief TeacherTube video on fractions as a beginning segment for a new math unit or playing a video on the water cycle before starting a new science unit on that topic will capture student interest in the topic. In fact, having a group of students seek out appropriate TeacherTube videos for a given instructional unit can be a great small-group assignment. Videos can be found on practically every topic one could imagine, and many are appropriate for every grade level. It is important to remember that this is a platform for sharing content. Teachers and students can and should upload their own resources (photos, videos, documents) to share, and once a video is available, students should be encouraged to watch it with their parents at home.

TeacherTube is now offering a link to Teacher Vision—an extensive teacher resource page. Teachers can search through thousands of lesson plans divided by grade level and subject. Printable materials are available for graphic organizers, assignments, quizzes, tests, and calendars, and these will enrich the learning experience.

Diigo

Diigo (www.diigo.com) is an online bookmarking service that has the power to transform research assignments in the classroom. By downloading the Diigo toolbar, students and teachers have the ability to find, analyze, and organize research on the Internet. Teachers initially create an educator account and are then guided through the process of creating student accounts or accounts for student groups. Once set up, students are able to access the account and work in the group by viewing online materials. Online resources are shared by the teacher so that students can see posts, highlights, bookmarked resources, and comments.

If a fifth-grade social studies class is studying a particular president, the teacher can find an article online about that president, highlight specific parts of the article, and post "online sticky notes" about the article. The students are then able to access the article, see the teacher's highlighted sections, and respond to the teacher's questions on the "sticky notes." During a thematic unit of study, teachers can organize numerous articles on the content for student review through the unit.

The Partnership for 21st Century Skills advocates that students achieve informational literacy—that they are able to manage information from a variety of sources, use the information accurately, and evaluate it critically (Ferriter & Garry, 2010; Kay, 2010; Partnership for 21st Century Skills, 2004). Diigo helps students master these skills by letting teachers display a variety of websites and resources and show students how to evaluate and question them critically via the sticky note function. Having students respond and post helps them use the information accurately in discussion. Using Diigo scaffolds Internet usage for students, teaching them how to analyze the abundance of information they are inundated with on the Internet.

Twitter

Twitter (www.twitter.com) is a microblogging service that allows users to send and read brief messages. These short messages (limited to only 140 characters or less) are called *tweets*, and these tweets are posted on the author's profile page. Users can sign up to follow another author, making it so the author's tweets show up on the user's own home page. Ultimately, when an author makes a tweet, it shows up on his profile page and the profile page of each follower. Although accessible via today's mobile communication devices, Twitter can also be used from a personal computer or laptop. Twitter is designed so that each tweet is made public; however, settings can be arranged so that only followers can access the information.

Although many people see Twitter as a place where people simply post what they ate for lunch and the workout they did at the gym, it can be a useful tool in education (List & Bryant, 2010). Teachers can use this service to extend the school day, engage students in course content, and encourage critical thinking of particular points in the homework assignment. Using Twitter for these purposes not only engages the students in a manner that most students are comfortable with, but also teaches students responsible uses of such social-networking services.

Teachers can use Twitter as a means of professional development because it allows for the quick exchange of ideas and help. Teachers can tweet about new lesson plan ideas, assessments, or successful unit plans. They can post requests for special speakers, share funny teaching stories, ask for book ideas, and tweet about useful resources (Cole, 2009). Teachers can even sign up to follow tweets from professional development organizations such as the Partnership for 21st Century Learning (www.p21.org).

Students as well as teachers will benefit from the use of Twitter in the classroom. One of the most obvious uses is instant communication, similar to using a class blog. Teachers can post short messages reminding students of upcoming assignments, quizzes, and homework. As students "follow" the teacher's tweets, they are visible on the student's homepage, again extending the school day by connecting teachers and students more directly using a venue students enjoy. Teachers can tweet links for students to check out, questions for students to reflect on, or simple notes of encouragement before test days.

To extend the use of Twitter beyond class communication, teachers may make Twitter an assignment on its own. Students might be required to follow famous people and report on their tweets. Students can be asked to give a summary of an assigned article read or piece of literature. The 140 character limit forces students to think critically and succinctly—delving into the most important information and summarizing it. See Box 2.1 for sample tweets a teacher might send out to students. Of course, teachers must be sensitive to accessibility. In classes where every student has a smartphone, Twitter can easily be used, but in other situations, teachers must make certain that students without smartphones access have access to a laptop in the classroom to complete such assignments.

TECHNOLOGY TOOLS FOR TEACHING, GRADING, AND EVALUATION

In today's world of data-based decision making, gathering and using evaluation data is an absolute requirement for every teacher. Each piece of data a

---

Box 2.1   **Sample Instructional Tweets**

- Don't forget, AP History quiz first thing in the morning!
- All students must turn in media release form before participating in wiki project
- Teachers—check out http://www.p21.org for a framework of media literacy skills
- Read Chapter 3 and write a short tweet detailing the turning point of the story
- Check out video on fractions http://www.teachertube.com/viewVideo.php?video_id=24266&title=Mr_Duey___Fractions_Official_Video
- Follow President Obama's tweets now through midterm election—will discuss in class
- What part of our lecture today was most interesting to you?
- Great work on quizzes—I'm impressed with the scores!
- SNOW! School is on two-hour delay!
- The class blog has been updated . . . check it out!
- Download this document on Solar System http://www.teachertube.com/viewArticle.php?article_id=62&title=Solar_System
- Refer to Solar System document to complete homework assignment

teacher obtains about a student can drive instructional decisions. As the RTI process described in Chapter 1 shows, frequent progress monitoring data show whether students have mastered information, as well as when particular students need further intervention. Data come in the form of weekly progress monitoring, benchmarks, end-of-year assessments, portfolios, and observations, and much of these data can be managed through judicious use of technology. Technology tools can help teachers gather, grade, evaluate, and store data so that instruction given is appropriately delivered for each child in the class. The technology available not only helps teachers organize data but also provides a variety of avenues for student evaluation—increasing student motivation and decreasing student anxiety.

> *Technology tools can help teachers gather, grade, evaluate, and store data so that instruction given is appropriately delivered for each child in the class.*

Webquests

Webquests provide an exciting opportunity for students to research content online in a "guided tour" format. In a webquest, students use prompts and links provided by the teacher to analyze and synthesize information on the Internet. Students are able to sift through information on a particular topic in a predictable order as predetermined by the teacher, thus scaffolding their learning and building their understanding of the content as they progress.

> *Using a webquest, students are able to sift through information on a particular topic in a predictable order, scaffolding their learning and building their understanding of the content as they progress.*

Webquests typically follow a basic format by providing the students with an introduction, task, resources, instructions, a conclusion, and a rubric or other evaluation tool. The introduction is intended to motivate students and get them excited about the assignment. The task section then helps students understand the objectives for the lesson and makes them aware of the final required product. Students then use the links provided along with the questions the teacher has posted on the webquest and work through information on the Internet in the selected resources section. In that sense, the webquest tasks provide "gates" to information after prerequisite tasks are completed. Questions may be answered on a paper handout or actually answered in an online format. The instruction section of a webquest goes through the detailed process students will take to complete the webquest. Finally, there is a conclusion that reiterates the purpose of the webquest and reminds the students of the objectives they were to meet. The evaluation is usually a rubric or grading scale that helps students know how their performance will be evaluated (Concept to Classroom, 2004). There are numerous sites available that help teachers create their own webquest for the classroom. See Box 2.2 for a list of available websites that present webquest templates.

Webquests operate in students' zones of proximal development and offer teachers a variety of opportunities for differentiation. Teachers can use links to material that is of a higher reading level for students who need extra challenge and links to material of a lower reading level for students needing intervention. Websites (e.g., http://juicystudio.com/

Box 2.2 **Useful Websites to Assist in Creating Webquests**

https://www.teachersfirst.com/summer/webquest/quest-a .shtml—This site provides a tutorial on creating webquests for the classroom, and in doing that tutorial, teachers can create a webquest they can subsequently use.

http://www.internet4classrooms.com/using_quest.htm—This website described five components of webquests including introduction, task description, process for completion, evaluation criteria and rubrics, and conclusion. Additional links are provided for development of webquests.

http://questgarden.com/—This website was created by Bernie Dodge, the developer of webquests. This site does require membership, which costs $20 for a two-year subscription. The site offers user-friendly templates for creating webquests and makes it easy to upload documents, images, and worksheets in the webquest. It also encourages users to "share" their work. Instead of creating a completely new webquest, teachers can use previously designed webquests and adapt them for their individual needs. A thirty-day free trial is available if teachers are interested in sampling the website before subscribing.

https://www.teacherweb.com/—Teacher web is another online tool that helps create webquests and web pages. The subscription costs $27 annually.

http://www.kn.pacbell.com/wired/fil/—This website offers free templates for creating webquests. Step-by-step instructions make it fairly simple for teacher use.

http://www.zunal.com/—This website is another webquest maker that does not require a subscription.

services/readability.php#readweb) are available to help teachers determine the readability of any website they might choose to include in a webquest.

Webquest enhances learning since using a webquest allows students to discover information on their own. Instead of sitting in a lecture or watching a class video, students use the guidance from the teacher to explore the information, making the learning more interactive. The links and questions scaffold the information as students practice their 21st-century learning skills and thus work to become independent lifelong learners. For students with academic challenges, webquests can be completed by pairs of students working through the content together. Guidance from the teacher also helps students understand appropriate uses of information on the Internet. A sample webquest is presented in Box 2.3.

Webquests are available and easily accessible for practically every content area. Students can use webquests to read various types of literature, to research historic events, and to delve into scientific information. These can be completed in the classroom, in the computer lab or media

---

Box 2.3   **Webquest on *Jungle Book***

This webquest is designed for a fifth-grade classroom as students work on an integrated unit based on their reading of the *Jungle Book* by Rudyard Kipling.

Introduction

You are Mowgli and you are taken in by a wolf family. During this webquest, you will use all that we have learned about the *Jungle Book* to put yourself in Mowgli's shoes. You should be thinking critically about his situation, his surroundings, and his life. You will then be able to compare and contrast particular settings, characters, and events in the story.

Task

With a partner, you will research an animal of your choosing. Then, you will create an online journal under the Mowgli "guise" and detail what life is like growing up with that particular animal. You will be sure to cover what you must eat, how you sleep, how you stay warm, how you defend yourself, and where you live. Just as Mowgli survived with the wolf family, now you must survive with your own animal of choosing.

Instructions

- Go through each of the resources to gather information on the animal you choose.
- Take notes on the information you think will be helpful in determining how Mowgli might have survived with your animal. Document your information.
- Create an online blog detailing life with this animal pack. Your blog must include two weeks worth of journal entries.
- Be sure your blog includes information on how Mowgli will eat, sleep, dress, and defend himself. Think critically about how Mowgli behaved in our study of the *Jungle Book* and be sure to include this type of behavior in your blog. Although he may be in a different setting with the animal of your choosing, Mowgli is still Mowgli.

Selected Resources

- http://kids.nationalgeographic.com/kids/animals/creaturefeature/
  - Use this site to pick your animal and find out information on your animal's habitat, diet, and survival methods.
  - http://www.kidsplanet.org/factsheets/map.html
  - This site will provide you with fact sheets on animals. Once you pick your animal, locate it on the map and find out information to help you "live" with the animal.
  - http://www.classchatter.com
  - Use our class blog page to create your own online journal.

Conclusion

I hope you have learned that a character is a multidimensional part of literature. I hope that the webquest made you think critically about the main character you have studied and helped you learn how to apply one part of a text to another situation. Remember all that you have learned as you read your next piece of literature—consider the possibilities with each character you encounter.

center, or even at home dependent on student resources. In particular, we recommend that every webquest be coupled with an evaluation rubric that delineates expectations about what students should accomplish in completing the webquest. Box 2.4 presents a sample webquest rubric for a fifth-grade literature class.

| Box 2.4 | A Webquest Evaluation Rubric |

The following rubric will help you as you complete your assignment.

4	• An animal was specified and chosen from the assigned resources
	• Organized notes were taken documenting extensive research from both resources and even several independent resources
	• More than fourteen blog entries were created
	• Blog entries mentioned animal habitat, diet, self-defense, and survival information
	• Relevant comparisons were made showing Mowgli's true character from the story
3	• An animal was specified and chosen from the assigned resources
	• Notes were taken documenting research from both resources
	• Fourteen blog entries were created
	• Blog entries mentioned animal habitat, diet, self-defense, and survival information
	• Relevant comparisons were made showing Mowgli's true character from the story
2	• An animal was specified and chosen from the assigned resources
	• Limited notes were taken documenting research from only one of the resources
	• Ten blog entries were created
	• Blog entries did not mention every required piece including animal habitat, diet, self-defense, and survival information
	• Loose comparisons were made showing Mowgli's true character from the story
1	• An animal was specified and chosen outside of given resource
	• No notes were turned in
	• Less than ten blog entries were created
	• Blog entries did not mention required material including animal habitat, diet, self-defense, and survival information
	• No comparisons were made showing Mowgli's true character from the story

> *We recommend that every webquest be coupled with an evaluation rubric that delineates expectations about what students should accomplish in completing the webquest.*

Glogster

Glogster EDU (edu.glogster.com) is an online web service that helps with the innovative expression of skills. Using Glogster, students and teachers can create virtual posters that are enhanced with multimedia to demonstrate knowledge of course content (Ojalvo & Schulten, 2010). Students choose from a variety of templates and follow simple step-by-step instructions to create their glog. Recommended by the *New York Times* Teaching and Learning Blog (Ojalvo & Schulten, 2010), Glogster creates a platform for creative student expression and generation of knowledge. Students can work independently or in small groups to create a multimedia presentation related to virtually any course content. Teachers might wish to have students create posters on new math facts, books they recently read, or science or social studies content.

Once students have finished a glog, the teacher can set the glog so that peers can review it and provide comments. All comments are monitored by the teacher. Glogs are private unless the teacher chooses to publish them, using a "public for all" setting that allows other teachers and students to view the work.

Glogster is accessed through a fee-for-service funding plan. Teachers can choose from a free Glogster basic membership or can opt to purchase a premium membership for around $60. By purchasing the premium membership, teachers are entitled to tech support, glogs without advertising, document-attachment features, class messaging, and direct access to student accounts. However, the free membership does include student account and glog management, comment and profile management, as well as video options. Students do not have to have their own personal e-mail account.

Glogster EDU provides a platform for student expression. Students are motivated to present research and group findings because they are able to create a virtual poster including text, graphics, animation, and video. Teachers can use glog assignments as final projects, assessments, and components of student portfolios for evaluation purposes. Glogster provides opportunities for differentiation by structuring the material in a variety of ways. It can also serve as an extension activity for advanced or gifted students who need extra challenge. Students seeking an extra challenge can be required to access higher-level content and use teacher provided websites to find more research on the course content.

Alternatively, it can serve as an intervention activity for students who need extra help. Students who are intimidated by the thought of writing a full-length research paper can begin their research presentation with a glog and then move into the research paper assignment. Glogster's short format style will help struggling readers and writers record concise facts in an interesting and exciting way. See Box 2.5 for a list of differentiated unit project ideas using Glogster.

TECHNOLOGY TOOLS FOR TEACHER AND STUDENT PUBLISHING

Effective communication has always been one goal of education, and most recently, the Partnership for 21st Century Skills framework requires that each student be able to communicate clearly using modern communication tools (Cote, 2007; Ferriter & Garry, 2010; Kay, 2010; Partnership for 21st Century Skills, 2007; Salend, 2009). This means that students must be able

---

Box 2.5 **Differentiated Ideas for a Jungle Book Unit**

These project ideas culminate a study of the *Jungle Book* by Rudyard Kipling in a fifth-grade literature class. To enhance student interest and to allow for differentiation, students were able to work in a small group to pick the unit project they wanted to complete. Each group was to present their findings via Glogster—creating a virtual poster to explain what they discovered in their research. All activities for each grade adhere to the National Anchor Standards 7, 8, and 9 for writing (www.corestandards.org). These standards indicate that students will

7. conduct short as well as more sustained research projects based on focused questions, demonstrating understanding of the subject under investigation;

8. gather relevant information from multiple print and digital sources, assess the credibility and accuracy of each source, and integrate the information while avoiding plagiarism; and

9. draw evidence from literary or informational texts to support analysis, reflection, and research.

Project 1: Final Product

- Students will create a glog that compares and contrasts their city/ life with the life/city of a child in present-day India.

Process

- Students will pick one city in India.
- With teacher guidance, they will research the city including topics such as
  - food,
  - clothing,
  - education,
  - housing, and
  - families.
- Students will then compare and contrast their life with the life of a child in their city.
- Students will create a glog to depict this information and present it.

Project 2: Final Product

- The group will choose one animal from the story. They will research the animal and the animal's habitat. They will then create a glog that depicts how they would have to "adapt" to live in the environment the animal lives in—just as Mowgli had to adapt. For instance, if they had to live with lions—what would they have to change?

Process:

- Students will pick one animal from the story.
- They will need to research
  - animal habitat,
  - feeding, and
  - how to protect themselves.
- They will then create a glog answering questions such as
  - What things would they embrace if they lived with the animal?
  - What things would they avoid?

Project 3: Final Product

- Students will create a glog that depicts what would happen if Mowgli was suddenly "transposed" into a different environment. Students will use his character from the story to gain insight into what he would do.

(Continued)

(Box 2.5 Continued)

Process:

- Students will choose another setting for Mowgli:
  - ○ Lost at sea
  - ○ At school
  - ○ In the arctic
  - ○ In a big city
- Each group will prepare a glog that depicts how Mowgli would react in these circumstances.
- Students will need to use Mowgli's behavior in *Jungle Book* as a guide so that the character stays "true" in whichever setting they choose

Project 4: Final Product

- Students will create a glog that depicts how today's technology tools would have impacted the story if Mowgli had had access to them.

Process

- Students are to think about the primitive life Mowgli lived.
- Research the "tools" the environment provided him.
- Discuss how Mowgli's life would be different if he had the technology available to him that we have. How could those "tools" change the outcome of the story?

to articulate their thoughts and ideas, whether that be orally, nonverbally, through written communication, or using modern presentation software. With that 21st-century goal in mind, it is imperative that teachers begin to access the technology tools that are available to help students achieve this goal. Using technology for student publishing helps students see end results when writing—they understand they have an audience and they must work to engage that audience. In today's society, students are constantly publishing via Facebook, MySpace, and their own personal blogs. It is now time to use these same tools in the classroom to teach the appropriate use of these publishing mediums (Ferriter & Garry, 2010; Kay, 2010; Wilmarth, 2010).

> *The Partnership for 21st Century Skills framework requires that each student be able to communicate clearly orally, nonverbally, through written communication, or using modern presentation software.*

Blogs

By offering a class blogging system, students are able to connect with teachers and students worldwide for discussions on any topic they desire. Blogs are similar to online journals with each posting being categorized by date (Bender & Waller, 2011; Ferriter & Garry, 2010). Those who read the blog are able to comment on the author's postings on that particular topic, thus making the blog similar to an interactive website on a particular topic. The social-networking sites available to students today demonstrate that most students appreciate and expect high levels of connectivity. Having a classroom blog takes advantage of the students' interest in being connected and teaches them the responsible uses of such interaction (Cote, 2007; Salend, 2009).

Blogs are becoming an increasingly popular medium of communication in the education world as they offer some advantages that cannot be overlooked. Simple journaling about the events of one's day or posting favorite links to a website is not considered blogging. Blogging is when there is synthesis and analysis of concepts. Blogging is considered to be a more formal exchange of ideas, and in that sense, blogging is reflective writing that offers links to other content. Thus, blogging is a slightly more formal medium for communication and a sharing of ideas than some of the tools previously discussed (Richardson, 2010).

> *Blogging is when there is synthesis and analysis of concepts; blogging is an exchange of ideas based on reflective writing that offers links to other content.*

The options for use of blogging in the classroom are practically endless (Cote, 2007; Salend, 2009). For teachers, it can be a way to communicate with other professionals—a way to share ideas, best practices, and encouragement for daily use in the classroom. In particular, we recommend that teachers review the website on blogging, Links to School Bloggers (http://supportblogging.com/Links+to+School+Bloggers), for a list. Links to School Bloggers provides an extensive list of educators who blog about their own personal experiences, and most of the blogs center around the use of technology in the classroom.

There are numerous other websites available that offer free blogs for teachers to use with their students. Teachers will need to search out a blog host that is suitable for their needs—some are ad free; some require login and password information. The authors of this book recommend using a password-protected blog to ensure heightened levels of security for your students. See Box 2.6 for a list of recommended education blogs.

Blogs can also help bridge the gap between school and home. Teachers can set up class blogs that are available for parent use and commentary. Class blogs can contain calendars, current events, homework, upcoming trips, and class reminders. To incorporate synthesis and analysis, class blogs can also contain reflections on class assignments, readings for parents that include up-to-date research, and invitations for parents to comment on issues that are being discussed in class (Richardson, 2010). While educators have long lamented the problems connecting with parents, technology such as classroom blogs may be one way to reach many busy parents who are used to connecting in online environments.

Box 2.6   Websites for Creating Secure Classroom Blogs

http://www.classblogmeister.com/—This is a free website that provides a template for teachers to create their own password-protected classroom blogs. Teachers in middle and high school may wish to create a semester-long blog and then vary the postings and topics based on particular units of instruction.

www.gaggle.net—Gaggle provides free or fee-based e-mail and blog tools for teachers and students. The site has numerous filters available that allow teachers to filter for inappropriate words and images, and teachers have control over who can post on the site.

http://www.21classes.com/—21 Classes is another blog option for teachers that offers several layers of protection for students in the class, including password protection and additional teacher controls. Teachers can moderate the comments and edit specific posts as necessary, prior to posting on the blog. A free version is available, as well as a fee-based version that offers higher levels of security.

http://education.weebly.com/—Weebly is a free resource for creating classroom websites and blogs. The education version allows for ad-free blogging, which is great for students. Teachers can set the blog to public or private—we recommend private so that a password is required for blog access. The private option heightens security for teachers and students.

www.classchatter.com—ClassChatter is a free service for creating classroom blogs. ClassChatter is ad free, but to keep costs low, they do not support the uploading of images or sound files. Teachers can create topic and assignment blogs, and students can create personal blogs. Teachers can edit any post. When students create their own personal blogs for reflection, they can be made available for the entire class or just the teacher. Also, teachers can create and grade assignments from the class blog.

Students across the public school grades will greatly benefit from the exchange of ideas via blogging, as long as basic reading and basic computer skills have been mastered. Teachers can set up class blogs where students respond to readings, posts, and links that correspond with the content being studied. Discussion assignments using a blog provide numerous opportunities for students who are not vocal in class to express themselves in a less intimidating way. Blogs also motivate students to publish work of a higher standard as they realize their work will be viewed by a much larger audience. Rather than writing a theme or research paper, for which the teacher would be the sole reader, a blog posting is read and reviewed by peers, and this often results in higher engagement with the assigned task when it is to be posted to the class blog. If the blog is public, student writing is available worldwide, which encourages students to truly consider their audience. Of course, only this type of widely available writing will truly prepare students for the 21st century.

Wikis

Using wikis in the classroom might scare some teachers! After all, Wikipedia is an online encyclopedia that anyone can digitally edit, and Wikipedia content certainly contains some errors in fact. Educators may wonder, how can such a tool be useful for students as they try to write valid, factually based research papers?

As teachers in the 21st century, it is important to think about how all technology can be used to benefit our students, and to do that, teachers must challenge their own belief systems. While Wikipedia and other wikis are websites that allow anyone to publish anything at anytime (Richardson, 2010), this is not as scary as it sounds! Not only can users publish, but they can also edit anyone else's content. This leads to an online, collaborative community of information providers, and most errors on Wikipedia are corrected within twenty-four hours or so.

Although Wikipedia is probably the most well known of all wikis, there are certainly many other wikis. For instance, there are wikis devoted to recipes, quotes, books, education, and travel. Again, the most exciting part about these pages is that any user can add in a favorite recipe, quote, book, or hotel to stay in. Even better, users can edit someone else's recipe if he or she forgets to add in the correct amount of sugar or does not have the oven set for the correct temperature. In that sense, these wikis are truly collaborative and usually self-correcting. Intense collaboration is key in creating a wiki.

Can this collaboration be useful in the classroom? Teaching students how to work together and sort through information and evaluate it using other sources is certainly a set of skills necessary in the 21st century. Since students are inundated with information on a daily basis, it is the responsibility of the teacher to teach students how to sift through information, evaluate its validity, determine the purpose of the author, and contribute their own findings and research to the digital world. Wikis provide the format to learn and apply these skills.

There are numerous ways to use wikis in the education arena. Schools can access Wetpaint (a wiki host) and create a wiki for their parent–teacher organization (PTO). The PTO wikis provide a forum for sharing school mission statements, posting calendars, and sharing pictures. However, the collaborative nature of a wiki allows users to update information on meetings, fund-raisers, and school events. Instead of waiting for the quarterly meeting, PTO members are able to collaborate throughout the school year without ever leaving their home.

Teachers and administrators can use wikis to share resources and ideas across districts and states. By accessing Teacher Peer Wikis (http://wikisineducation.wetpaint.com/page/Teacher+Peer+Wikis), teachers can choose from a variety of wikis that pertain to their grade level and subject level. There are wikis for teachers trying to create literacy centers, teachers trying to use more technology, even teachers teaching Japanese. Once a teacher chooses a wiki that pertains to his or her level, the teacher can read the information there, post and edit other teachers' information, and see how others edit their information. Wikis create an environment in which teachers can collaborate at any time during the day or school year, instead of waiting for one professional development day to discuss their ideas.

Teachers and administrations will surely benefit from learning how to create and share wikis with their colleagues. However, students have much to gain from learning these important skills as well. Students can create their own wiki pages to share project information and research. Wetpaint is a company that hosts wikis and provides easy to use templates to help students get started. See Box 2.7 for steps on how to create a wiki.

If a class is working on the solar system, a teacher may create eight small groups and assign a planet to each one. As students research and learn, their final project would be to create a wiki on their planet, including any relevant information discovered. Once the wiki is created, other class members can access the page and edit the information. A class member from the Earth group may add in up-to-date information heard in class lectures or read in-class assignments on the Mercury wiki. Discussion links provided on wiki pages allow users to communicate about changes. The interconnectivity of wikis helps students publish their own work, think critically about others' work, and learn to manage and modify using constructive criticism. These are all important skills that students must attain before entering the workplace in the 21st-century world.

Having students create wikis for collaborative projects is a great use of the resource. However, teachers can also use wikis to create ongoing resources for their classroom. By creating a class wiki, teachers and

> **Box 2.7** **How to Create a Wiki**
>
> There are many places that offer templates for wiki creation; however, this step-by-step guide accompanies a wiki started at www.wikispaces.com. Wikispaces provides free, private wikis for educators.
>
> - To begin, access http://www.wikispaces.com/site/for/teachers.
>
> - Once this site is accessed, teachers will need to prepare a username, password, and a wikispace name.
>
> - Teachers must decide if the wiki should be public (where anyone can view and edit), protected (everyone can view, but only members can edit), or private (only wiki members can view and edit). To begin, it is suggested that teachers use the private option which is free for educators.
>
> - Once the page is established, wiki spaces will offer a wiki tutorial to help with set up.
>
> - Users are instructed to use the "edit this page" tab to work with text, fonts, and spacing.
>
> - Each time a new page is created, teachers should link to that page by highlighting the text and clicking the Earth icon.
>
> - Images and files can be uploaded by clicking on the icon that looks like a tree in a box.
>
> - Teachers can invite students and parents to join the wiki using the "user creator" feature. Student and parents do not have to have an e-mail account to be a member of the wiki site.

students can cowrite and coedit class specific textbooks. Teachers can post articles and information and allow students to contribute and edit each other's information. Students can upload images, videos, and journal entries. When the semester is over, the wiki would be available as a starting point for the next group of students (Richardson, 2010).

The idea of putting student work on a wiki for anyone to see and edit can be daunting for educators, but as they get used to the process, it becomes much less stressful. For security purposes, teachers should access and use wikis that require logins and passwords. This helps "gate" the community that has access to the wiki and will help safeguard students and students' work. However, teachers should keep in mind that students are typically more motivated when they realize their work is being viewed by a larger audience, so over-restriction on student publications is not desirable.

> *Teachers should keep in mind that students are typically more motivated when they realize their work is being viewed by a larger audience.*

Teachers would also benefit from becoming familiar with www.curriki .org. This is a free online website that offers open-source material for teachers from kindergarten through Grade 12. The name, Curriki, is a play on the words curriculum and wiki. Curriki offers lesson plans in all subject areas for teachers to browse by subject or standards. Curriki also provides opportunity for teachers to connect with each other. They can give and get constructive feedback on lessons and units and join new groups to share ideas and existing curriculum.

Wikis are similar to blogs in several ways, but from the instructional point of view, there are important differences. Box 2.8 delineates several differences for teachers to consider when using these newly emerging tools for instruction.

Podcasts

Podcasts are digital audio files that can be heard via classroom computers, iPods, and MP3 players. Podcasts are single subject episodes with information presented in a format similar to a radio talk show. Teachers can access created podcasts via the Internet to aid in the presentation of information in the classroom. Podcasts are available on every

---

Box 2.8   What's the Difference Between a Blog and a Wiki?

Blogs and wikis have some commonalities. Both are websites where files and links can be uploaded. Blogs and wikis allow for posting and even discussion. However, there are a few distinct differences that distinguish a weblog from a wiki. Blogs are typically updated by one user; wikis are created to be updated by any user at anytime. A wiki is continually changing as users edit and collaborate; a blog consists of one user posting and a reader commenting. Wiki .answers.com states that a blog is "one-to-many communication," whereas a wiki is "many-to-many" communication.

When choosing between a blog and a wiki in the classroom, consider the primary purpose. If looking to have a site where information is easily accessed and modified, consider using a wiki. For instance, a wiki would be best for trying to create an online textbook for a class, where students update and edit content information. A blog is more limited in terms of editing and modification. If a teacher is looking to create a site where students respond to a particular post or thought, she would be better served using a blog.

If a social studies teacher wants to get students thinking on the Civil War, she may post an introductory comment on the class blog and ask for student reflections. Students can post their own thoughts, respond to the teacher's original entry, and respond to each other. Once the class begins researching and learning about the Civil War, she may have them contribute their findings to the class wiki. Students would be able to update and edit each other's pages creating an ongoing resource for the classroom.

topic imaginable and typically can be downloaded for free. Teachers can search and use podcasts to pique student interest in a new unit of study, thus using the podcast as an interest grabber on the first day of the unit. For instance, when studying the Civil War, teachers can play the podcast of Abraham Lincoln's speech (http://kids.learnoutloud.com/Kids-Free-Stuff/History/-/Gettysburg-Address/16984) or access the Aesop's Fables podcast (http://kids.learnoutloud.com/Kids-Free-Stuff/Literature/World-Classics/Aesops-Fables-Podcast/23064#plink) when starting a new literature unit. Again, the majority of these podcasts are free for teacher use. See Box 2.9 for websites with podcasts available for free downloads.

Students become even more interested in their lessons when they are allowed to create their own podcasts. Researching, writing, editing, and publishing their own podcast encourages students to become intricately involved with the content matter. A fifth-grade teacher in North Carolina studying the American Revolution may divide students into small research groups. One group may research and edit a podcast discussing possible causes and effects of the American Revolution, one group may present a podcast on the Boston Massacre, another may study the Battle of Guilford Courthouse (a significant action that took place in NC), and another might study the British Southern Campaign ending in Yorktown and Patriot victory. Each group could be responsible for gathering, synthesizing, and editing information to publish a creative podcast for their peers, or the class could consider a project in which the various presentations were put together for publishing. As with various technologies discussed previously, students are more motivated to participate in this type of in-depth interaction with the content when they are able to use the technology they enjoy and publish their work for a larger audience (Wilmarth, 2010). Podcasts can also be used to present class material to absent peers, to report on current events, and to share research papers.

> **Box 2.9** **Websites That Feature Podcasts for Instruction**
>
> www.learnoutloud.com/—This site features a link to help teachers learn how to access podcasts, as well as a podcast directory for teachers to assist in finding podcasts for educational use. Most podcasts are free, but some access options such as iTunes may require accounts for accessing podcasts.
>
> http://epnweb.org/—The Education Podcast Network is a website that has numerous podcasts for teachers broken down by subject area. There is also a catalog of podcasts created by students that will give teachers an idea of how podcasts can be used in their classroom. As always, teachers should carefully listen to the entire podcast prior to using a podcast in the classroom.
>
> http://audacity.sourceforge.net/—Audacity provides free software for recording and editing sounds, which can be of use in teacher-created or student-created podcasts.
>
> http://grammar.quickanddirtytips.com/default.aspx— Grammar Girl offers weekly podcasts for older students on tricky grammar rules, which can assist in a variety of reading and language arts areas. It is a fun way to get students thinking about their writing and their speech. Teachers can subscribe to the podcast through the website.

The tools necessary for creating classroom podcasts are minimal. Teachers and students will need a personal computer, an appropriate microphone, and Internet access. There are websites available that provide free editing software. Although editing is not essential, it does make the podcast more professional and allows for more interaction with the content being edited.

Once created, podcasts can be uploaded to class blogs as well as student and class wikis. Student-created podcasts can then serve as review material, available for the entire semester for every student. The long-term effectiveness of podcasts cannot be overlooked.

Of course, with student-created work, teachers must consider the security prior to posting podcasts. No student identification information should be provided, and in many schools, it may be required that podcasts be posted only on blogs and wikis that require school-controlled logins and passwords. As with the other instructional technologies discussed in this chapter, we recommend always securing the permission of parents and the administration before posting any student-created podcasts.

Animoto

Animoto (www.animoto.com) is an online service committed to creating videos from each user's images and video clips. There are three levels of membership: a basic free membership that creates thirty-second videos; an all-access membership for $30 a year that allows for full-length videos; and the pro membership meant for businesses and corporations. With Animoto, a user simply uploads images and short video clips, picks a background, picks a soundtrack, and clicks edit. Instantly, Animoto creates a video from these images. Users can add text as well to make the video tell a story or present specific content. The website is extremely user friendly and needs minimal input before creating a professional video.

> *Animoto is an online service committed to creating videos from each user's images and video clips.*

In a few short minutes, teachers using Animoto can create a video that gives parents a glimpse into the classroom. For example, if a class of sixth-grade students is studying the rainforest, teachers can take pictures from the Internet, pictures of students' class projects, and a few short video segments featuring student presentations and upload all of those images to Animoto. The result is a professional-looking video that chronicles that unit of study. Once the video is complete, Animoto makes it easy to upload the video directly to class blogs for viewing. Now, parents are able to actually see what the students are doing in their class projects. In essence, teachers are creating online photo and video galleries.

WHICH TECHNOLOGY TOOLS SHOULD I USE?

By now, most readers will realize that this chapter could have easily been expanded by discussion of many more instructional ideas, based on modern communications technologies and other instructional tools. In fact, this chapter has only scratched the surface in discussing these tools, and given this daunting array of instruction tools, teachers might wonder how they might begin or what tools they might use for a given instructional task.

As teachers begin to move into the brave new world of instruction made possible by these ever-changing technologies, there are several suggestions we can make. Given that these technologies are constantly evolving, educators should realize that no teacher will ever truly be an expert in all of these instructional approaches. Rather than feel intimidated by this array of teaching tools, we recommend that teachers begin with relatively simple technologies that they might be familiar with in their everyday lives. If teachers have a Facebook page personally, they should be quite comfortable establishing such a page for their instructional needs. However, for teachers not yet using Facebook, we don't recommend an immediate jump into uncharted territory. Rather, they should use a technology that they are already using personally, perhaps increased Internet usage or increased use of instructional software that is already used at the school.

Next, teachers should consider the technologies that are supported by resources at their school. If Smart Boards, presentation software, and Internet capability are available in the classroom, then begin with those tools and get some experience in using those first. Under those conditions, we'd recommend that teachers leave the webquests and wikis alone for a few months. Those tools might be explored during the next semester or next year. Of course, teachers will also want to consider what online instructional resources might be available to them given their particular subject area. Also, teachers might consider the technologies used by other teachers in their building. Would those teachers share some expertise in using those instructional tools? Moving into technology applications based on what is available, what technologies schools support, and what technological help one might have from the teacher across the hallway is certainly appropriate in this new instructional world.

Finally, consideration of what types of technology tools and instructional approaches are appropriate for a given subject is recommended. For example, the Internet, while wholly ungoverned, may have much more content that could assist in studies of U.S. history than, say, Latin or advanced physics (of course, even in those subjects, the Internet sources would be nearly boundless). Still, consideration of what tools lend themselves to the types of tasks associated with study of a given area is warranted, and as teachers become more fluent in these tools, such considerations will become second nature. To illustrate this point, Box 2.10 presents some guidelines on what teaching tools might be appropriate for given types of tasks.

CREATING A TECHNOLOGY-FRIENDLY CLASSROOM

To use all of the technology-based differentiation strategies heretofore mentioned, teachers must have classrooms that are technology friendly—classrooms that are equipped with the tools necessary to carry out these projects and ideas. It is important to remember that each step toward a 21st-century classroom is a positive step (Kay, 2010), though with funding tighter than ever, it can be difficult to acquire any new hardware for classrooms. Still, it is essential that teachers and administrators work together

Box 2.10   **Which Technology Should I Use?**

- If you want to create a place for parents to connect with the classroom, consider a classroom blog. Parents can respond to posts made by the teacher and view current classroom happenings.
- If you want to create a place for students to interact with content after the school day, consider a class wiki. Students can collaborate on group projects, track changes to their own work, and discuss any changes that are to be made. Teachers can elect to be notified of any changes on the wiki to track student involvement and participation.
- If you want to create a place that will contain lasting, content-specific resources, use a wiki. Students and teachers can edit information in a continuous format. These changes are saved and can be used as a starting place for information for a new group of students.
- If you want to create a sense of classroom community, try the class blog. The interaction between posts and comments will help learners get to know their peers in an open, friendly environment.
- If you want to create a forum for pre- and post-class discussion, consider creating a class blog. Entries will be organized from the most recent post, making it easy to follow along with class happenings and topics.
- If you want a one-stop website that allows for posting, uploading links and files, tracking assignments, organizing grades, and individual and group discussions, use www.edmodo.com.
- If you are looking for a fun way to get students involved with content material for a presentation or an assignment, try having them create a podcast or a virtual poster on Glogster EDU. Creating a podcast or virtual poster not only motivates students; it also creates lasting review material. Upload the podcast or virtual poster to your class blog or website and you have review material for the entire class.
- If you want to create forms and quizzes for students and parents to fill out online, use Google Docs and embed the form in your class wiki.

to make it happen—the lifelong success of our students may very well depend on their digital communication skills in the 21st-century world. While it is impossible to describe all of the hardware that would benefit classrooms, what follow are a few of the pieces of hardware each classroom should contain to carry out fundamental technology integration.

Instructional Hardware

We recommend that every classroom have at least four computers with Internet access. If the district is not able to purchase computers for every classroom, mobile carts that hold four to six computers can be created for sharing among teachers. These computers are needed for students to work on modern software-based instruction, to complete group projects on the World Wide Web, and to complete many modern assessments.

The need for Internet access is critical; such access allows for the use of many more resources in the classroom and also provides the opportunity for more extensive student investigation and research. Modern education simply requires Internet access; without access to the Internet, students are not able to participate in class blogs, hear podcasts, create glogs, or perform webquests. Secure, reliable Internet access is a must for a technology-friendly classroom.

> *Modern education simply requires Internet access.*

It is also helpful for each classroom to have an interactive projection system such as a Smart Board, Promethean Board, or some other type of interactive whiteboard. Having an interactive whiteboard hooked up to a computer enables a teacher to project the work from the computer onto the large screen for the entire class to view. When introducing the class to the blog site, teachers can walk the students through the site while it is projected, answering questions and familiarizing the students with the layout. When assigning the creation of a class glog, teachers can take students to Glogster and walk them through each step to avoid later confusion during their individual creation. Using these projection systems, teachers can project podcasts to open a new unit and TeacherTube videos to introduce a new concept. Students can also use the projection to present their own PowerPoints, podcasts, and glogs so that the entire class can see their final product.

The interactive component of the whiteboard enhances lessons and motivates students. A second-grade teacher introducing a lesson on patterns can create shapes on the whiteboard and have students come forward and manipulate them into the pattern stipulated while other students create the same pattern with shape manipulatives on their desks. No longer do students have to observe a two-dimensional pattern in a textbook when studying a three-dimensional world; the shapes are now moveable in their classroom on their screen.

Another way to increase connectivity in the classroom is to purchase classroom response systems. Commonly called *clickers*, these game-like devices encourage active learning, provide immediate feedback of student understanding, and allow students to participate anonymously without fear of embarrassment (Martyn, 2007; Salend, 2009). Students use a handheld device to answer questions, the answers are wirelessly transmitted, and the class answers are presented on a teacher screen. Typically, answers are presented in a class graph so that the teacher can quickly analyze the data and use that data to drive instruction, determining when more explanation might be necessary. Graphs can display individual student answers, whole-group responses, or even subgroups within the class. Clickers simulate a video game, and this idea motivates students to participate in each question and discussion (Martyn, 2007).

Ideally, students in a technology-friendly classroom would have a 1:1 ratio: one student to one laptop. This has been referred to as the one-to-one initiative in various districts around the nation (Bender & Waller, 2011). In some cases, parents are encouraged to purchase a laptop for their children, and schools may provide some financial assistance for some students in that regard. In other cases, schools merely structure a mechanism to assure student access to a laptop while they are in the school building. As we move further into the 21st century, one might well anticipate that all students will need to have access to a laptop.

However, with budget cuts at an all-time high, schools have to seek reasonable alternatives to purchasing a computer for every student, and there are options available. Renaissance Learning Inc., as one example, markets a small word-processing device with some computer capability called the Neo2 Board (http://www.renlearn.com/neo/NEO2/#). This board is available for $149 and offers some excellent options for connectivity in the classroom. Toolbars can be added so that students can practice math facts, complete assessments, edit their writing, increase keyboarding skills, and take various assessments.

Neo2 can also be integrated with other tools already in the classroom such as desktop computers and whiteboards. The individualized components of Neo2 Boards align with the RTI pyramid, making it possible for students to receive personalized practice while teachers are able to routinely perform progress monitoring assessments for Tier 2 and Tier 3 interventions using that platform.

BRINGING "OUTSIDE" TECHNOLOGY "IN"

A technology-friendly classroom can also be a place where "outside" technology is welcomed. Districts can provide computers, Internet access, Neoboards, Smart Boards, and clickers, but sometimes it is important to consider the technology students already have and are already using. Although personal laptop computers are desired, there is also an endless variety of mobile Internet devices, most with some computing power, that are currently available (Manzo, 2010b).

Mobility Devices

Mobility devices such as cell phones are excellent resources for increasing student motivation, as they capitalize on the resources and tools the students already have. There are many reasons for using cell phones in the classrooms: students are already familiar with the device, they are inexpensive and convenient, and they offer applications such as cameras and touch screens. Cell-phone computers allow for twenty-four-hour-a-day connectivity and increase the amount of learning beyond the school day. Using cell-phone computers in the classroom increases technology skills while also teaching students responsible ways to use technology at home and at school (Gross & Spurka, 2010).

It is up to the teacher to decide how to use these devices to increase student motivation and achievement. Still, students do seem to be quite motivated to involve themselves with these new communications technologies, and the possibilities for use of these tools in education are virtually endless. It is important now to realize that technology is essential, not an add-on to the lesson. Further, the technology tools are not to be seen as the curriculum; they are to be seen as a way for the students to engage with the curriculum in a more meaningful way (Gross & Spurka, 2010).

> *Students do seem to be quite motivated to involve themselves with the new communications technologies, and the possibilities for use of these tools in education are virtually endless.*

Teachers have unlimited options when choosing to integrate mobile devices in the curriculum. For example, in the North Carolina Standard Course of Study, students in third grade are to "use appropriate vocabulary to compare, describe, and classify two- and three-dimensional figures." Using cell-phone computers, teachers might address that educational standard by having students complete a team scavenger hunt around the school, taking pictures of sample figures with their smartphones. Once back in the room, teams of students would be able to look at the sample picture taken and replicate it through drawing to share their content with the class. Students with advanced technology skills would also be able to upload the sample figures to a class blog and share the content with the class.

In a social studies classroom, teams of students might use their phones to video a reenactment of a particular historical event such as a political debate or speech. Once completed, teams would upload their videos to a shared site for all classmates to view. Incorporating this technology in the lesson would not only increase student motivation but also provide excellent review material. If students only performed these reenactments in class, those role-play examples would be limited to one viewing when the role-play was conducted. However, with the various videos uploaded to the blog, students would be able to refer to the material countless times before any exam. The connectivity that the cell phone provides increases the amount of time a student has to access any content material (Wilmarth, 2010).

At the Craik School in Canada, teachers used cameras on their cell phones to monitor group discussions. As students worked in literature circles, they recorded their group discussion and then used the Bluetooth software to send the video to the teacher's phone. This enabled the teacher to see and evaluate every minute of every group's discussion (Rapp, 2009), even though the teacher was not present when the students were holding the discussion.

The uses of a cell-phone computer are endless in the classroom as teachers employ creative techniques. However, the mobile devices are beneficial outside of the classroom as well. Project K-Nect in North Carolina provides an example of how these mobile devices increase 21st-century learning skills while also addressing the content. Funded by a grant from Qualcamm, Project K-Nect targets high school students in rural North Carolina who have limited math proficiency, and limited or no computer or Internet access at home.

According to Project K-Nect (2010), students are already part of the digital world and are curious as to how that digital work can become a part of their education. The program allows teachers to allocate a particular set of math problems aligned with North Carolina's Standard Course of Study. The problems begin with a short video that demonstrates the problem. Students work through the problem on their smartphones. If they cannot solve the problem, they are able to access their peers and collaborate on solving the problem. Once they return to solve the problem, the answer is submitted to the teacher. Students will then be allocated another problem that requires the same skill set to ensure mastery and prevent cheating. The smartphone provides twenty-four-hour help as students work together to master the curriculum content. Students participating in the project are encouraged to record their solutions on a blog and comment on their peers' posts. This not only promotes shared learning but also provides a less intimidating platform of communication for some students who may be less likely to participate in class discussions. Further, learning in this venue is extended in time well beyond the school day, and the device provides immediate academic assistance for each student virtually around the clock.

It is important for teachers to see the available resources that are compatible with mobile devices in the classroom. For instance, by subscribing to Poll Everywhere (www.polleverywhere.com), teachers are able to ask students a question and students respond via text messaging through their mobile device. The answers are then embedded on the teacher's webpage or in the teacher's PowerPoint presentation. Teachers can look at the results to instantly assess student understanding and use this information to inform instruction. A basic Poll Everywhere plan is free, or teachers can subscribe to a cost service to receive additional advanced options. Using software such as Poll Everywhere is another way to use 21st-century tools in a way that increases the depth of student knowledge in content areas.

Handheld Media Devices

Teachers across the country are using iPods, iPads, smartphones, PSPs, and MP3 players in the classroom (Ash, 2010; Davis, 2010a; Manzo, 2010b). For example, in the Grand Prairie schools in Texas, teachers are creating songs about scientific content for their students to listen to on their individual iPods, creating videos about the Solar System for students to watch, and downloading podcasts related to course content. Advocates of the program in this district say that the use of the iPods in the classroom is engaging student in a more meaningful way with the curriculum content (Chavez, 2007).

> *Teachers across the country are using iPods, iPads, smartphones, PSPs, and MP3 players in the classroom, and they report that these tools engage students in a more meaningful way with the curriculum content.*

When considering the use of these emerging instructional tools, it becomes clear that the phrase *revolution in the classroom* is not an overstatement. Teachers around the world are being forced to think how the "noneducational" technologies fit into the education setting (Manzo, 2010a). Although the use of these mobile devices is still under study, early research documents promising results, showing that there is an increase in achievement, student engagement, and motivation; improved attendance; and a reduction in discipline problems and dropout rates (Manzo, 2010a, 2010b).

Although this research is new and tentative, it can surely be stated that these technologies are and will be changing the classroom and education over the next decade. These personal-communication technologies offer endless differentiation options making it possible for teachers to deliver effective, personalized instruction for each student, long after the last bell rings. Teachers must stay current in application of these new teaching tools in the classroom and update their skills as necessary for using these emerging technologies to prepare their students for the 21st century.

STUDENT SECURITY IN THE DIGITAL WORLD

With the influx of technology in classrooms, security is a critical concern for every educator. Several times in this chapter, we have made recommendations for increased security in the digital teaching environment. As teachers seek to create a safe environment of connectivity using these new technologies, they must also teach their students responsible uses of the technology available to them. Teachers must always exercise caution when using the Internet as part of their instructional process, and teach their students to exercise the same cautions in using the digital communications technologies. Careful planning, including previewing, should be undertaken when using Internet resources such as YouTube, TeacherTube, and podcasts. When selecting websites for webquests, teachers should visit and evaluate their validity before assigning them for student research. We recommend that teachers search for and use ad-free websites so that inappropriate content is not shown at any point on the page or search.

Blogs, wikis, and class websites are important tools to use for connectivity, but all of these tools must be used with caution. Teachers can use the list of secure blogs mentioned previously that require passwords for entrance. This helps to ensure that the people looking and reading the blogs and wikis are truly invited. Even with secure blogs, students should never post any personal information such as last names, telephone numbers, addresses, or even school locations (Ferriter & Garry, 2010). If teachers or students are posting pictures of students in an educational activity, we recommend that a media release form be signed by student guardians prior to such posting.

We also recommend that teachers monitor any and all digital communications that students have in the context of their assignments. This is not that difficult to accomplish using blogs and other tools that are structured to allow for classroom use and teacher monitoring. Teaching students about these safeguards not only protects them while in the classroom but also teaches them appropriate uses of the Internet in their social lives as well.

As early as 2008 and 2009, various reports had circulated about cyberbullying and sexting, and the damage that could be done to young persons engaged in misuse of these communications tools. Educators, along with parents, across the nation became concerned as several stories of suicide resulting from cyberbullying received national attention. While these national media stories deal with noneducational applications of various communications technologies (i.e., Facebook pages, Internet posting, or students' private use of cell phones for photographs), these examples do illustrate that misuse of modern communications technology is dangerous. As these tools are increasingly used in the educational environment for instruction, educators must be vigilant and attend to students' safety and security at every step of the process.

However, these student security issues should not prohibit schools from seeking ways to apply this technology (Ferriter & Garry, 2010; Kay, 2010; Wilmarth, 2010). In fact, we believe that not using these modern teaching tools would be a grave mistake that would negatively impact the well-being of future generations of students. Further, we are confident that the security issues can be managed to assure student safety. The simple principles delineated herein will provide teachers with an initial set of security guidelines.

MEDIA LITERACY

Coupled with students' security in the digital environment is the concept of media literacy. In one sense, media literacy includes personal safety in use of modern technologies, and we believe that students must be trained to monitor their own security in this modern digital world. Further, it is possible that student self-awareness is the strongest tool we have for assuring students' safety.

However, media literacy reaches far beyond merely appropriate use of technologies. With the plethora of information available to students at each turn, teachers are responsible for instructing students on how to evaluate, critique, and interpret any information found on the Internet (Ferriter & Garry, 2010; Gregory & Kuzmich, 2005; Partnership for 21st Century Skills, 2007, 2009a). A high skill level in these areas results in a tech-savvy, highly independent consumer of digital media information, which in turn results in increased safety for students.

Schools have been using the Internet in classrooms for a number of years, and virtually every school is already emphasizing skills in evaluation and interpretation of digital information found on the Internet (Baker, 2008; Gregory & Kuzmich, 2005; Kay, 2010; Partnership for 21st Century Skills, 2009b). Of course, as more technologies get introduced in the classroom, these skills will need to be stressed for every technology. To be considered "literate" in information, communication, and technology skills, students must know how to evaluate information from a variety of sources critically and competently (Kay, 2010; Partnership for 21st Century Skills, 2004) and to use that information creatively in problem solving. Students should be taught to constantly question the validity of what they are reading, the strength of the source, the purpose of the author, and the overall authenticity of the information. With the abundance of information available to students, they must also learn to conduct extensive searches, compare information from one source to another, and make accurate evaluations of the sources (Gregory & Kuzmich, 2005).

The ability to think critically about the information found on the Internet is vital for student success in the 21st century, and this ability correlates nicely with several of the imaginings discussed in the introduction to this book. In the next century, knowledge will probably not be measured by merely memory tasks but rather by one's ability to obtain information, evaluate it, interpret it, compare it with other information from other sources, synthesize all of the information into a cohesive new understanding, and then use that newly generated understanding to solve problems. This set of skills will be the measure of success in the 21st century (Ferriter & Garry, 2010; Kay, 2010; Wilmarth, 2010).

Students must understand that all digital media (if not all media) are intentionally constructed for one purpose or another, usually involving profit or political power (Baker, 2008). Knowing that simple fact allows teachers and students to study the perspective of the author or creator of the media to ascertain his or her reasons for producing the media and thereby to more effectively evaluate the accuracy and value of the media product (Baker, 2008).

Knowing one's own media literacy is also advisable, and a simple self-evaluation can assist teachers and students in understanding their own media literacy. Teachers can use a form such as the one in Box 2.11. Teachers might wish to use this form or something similar to encourage students to reflect on their level of media literacy to develop critical-thinking skills among their students, thus preparing them for independent Internet research and analysis.

MODERN SOFTWARE-BASED INSTRUCTION

As use of technology increases, students are likely to do more of their learning using modern instructional software, and today software programs are available for almost any content in the traditional school

---

Box 2.11   Media Literacy Self-Evaluation Form

Name: _____   Date: _____   School: _____

Please indicate your skill level by circling one number for each indicator. 1 = can't or don't do this; 2 = do this sometimes; 3 = do this routinely. Then add all the scores together; the higher your total score, the higher your skill level.

Communication and 21st-Century Technology Skills			
I use text messaging	1	2	3
I have a Facebook page or MySpace page	1	2	3
I download music to some type of personal mobile device	1	2	3
I have done blogging	1	2	3
I use a smartphone, iPhone, or similar device	1	2	3
I have used online news sources	1	2	3
I evaluate my own work prior to sharing it with others	1	2	3

(Continued)

(Box 2.11 Continued)

Searching Skills			
I usually identify one or more keywords for searching	1	2	3
I use Google and other search tools	1	2	3
I use Wikipedia	1	2	3
I can refine my search using more exact terminology	1	2	3
I use complex searching or refined search functions in my online searches for information	1	2	3
I seek multiple online sources to understand the content	1	2	3
I always note if information is current in searching	1	2	3
I can use indexes, governmental sites, and online libraries for researching particular topics	1	2	3
I can describe the strengths/weaknesses of search engines	1	2	3
Organization and Interpretation of Information Skills			
I quickly skim/scan through information online	1	2	3
I jot down relevant websites as I search for information	1	2	3
I use outlining functions online to assist in organization of information as I find it	1	2	3
I seek to build an argument either pro or con, using the information I find online	1	2	3
I use PowerPoint, spreadsheets, or other software to help me organize information as I do a search	1	2	3
I can create heading, categories, and subsections for interpreting information as I find it	1	2	3
I revise and refine information prior to presenting it to others	1	2	3
Evaluation of Information Skills			
I evaluate sources and understand which types of information are more reliable	1	2	3
I look for contradictions and explore them relative to different sources of information	1	2	3
I can describe the difference between information found online, information found in a reputable newspaper, and information verified by a verdict in a court of law	1	2	3

I try to determine the author's purpose and author's viewpoint for information I find on the Internet	1	2	3
I seek primary as well as secondary sources of information	1	2	3
I seek contradictory viewpoints online to understand all sides of an issue	1	2	3
I evaluate the results of my own Internet search or any information I may generate based on the search	1	2	3

curricula. Thus, modern software-based curricula provides an avenue for instruction for nontraditional students who may need to work full-time during the day, as well as for individualized instructional interventions in the 21st-century classroom. It is vital that administrators and teachers make software instruction available as some students seem to respond to this instructional option more so than any other type of intervention (Bender & Waller, 2011).

Many of the modern software-based programs today can self-tailor questions and activities as students work through them, creating harder questions as students excel and providing short, intensive intervention examples when necessary. Often, teachers can select particular strands of content material for student practice and the programs indicate when mastery is reached. These programs typically provide detailed reports and can be extremely useful for benchmarking and progress monitoring during RTI procedures. Of course, the list of available programs is extensive; however, the authors have chosen several programs to discuss so that administrators and teachers are able to see the possibilities for their classrooms.

> *Modern software-based curriculum also provides an avenue for intensive, individualized instructional interventions in the 21st-century classroom.*

The SuccessMaker Curriculum

SuccessMaker is instructional software developed by Pearson Learning that provides individualized instruction for elementary and middle school students. SuccessMaker is a supplemental program and addresses the core subjects of reading and math. Students take an initial universal assessment, and the curriculum places the students in specific subjects at appropriate levels. As students complete the lessons, the levels and questions get increasingly complex to move students toward mastery.

In addition, SuccessMaker generates a variety of reports for teachers on how individual students are doing in their lessons. The reports make it possible to review student growth individually, in subgroups, or for the entire class. This makes it an excellent option for RTI implementation as teachers are able to closely monitor student performance and growth, and see the degree to which one student is succeeding compared with others in the class. Of course, like most computer-based instructional programs, students needing a Tier 2 or Tier 3 intervention are able to work with SuccessMaker on an individual basis, at their own pace, with a customized program.

Compared to other software-based instruction, research on SuccessMaker is somewhat more extensive. The What Works Clearinghouse listed thirty-six different research studies supportive of SuccessMaker. These studies showed the overall efficacy of the program in a variety of areas. (You can see that research review at http://ies.ed.gov/ncee/wwc/reports/adolescent_literacy/successmaker/references.asp.)

Study Island

Study Island (www.studyisland.com) is a web-based program that was created to match each state's standards in all areas tested on the state-wide assessments from third through eighth grade and high school. It is intended as a supplemental program designed to assess students' knowledge in the area designated by the teacher. It also offers testing preparation for kindergarten through second grade in math and reading; fine arts, health, and technology in elementary and middle school; and Algebra 2 mastery skills in high school. Study Island is available to licensed users anywhere that Internet is available, which makes it possible for students to work from home. That might be a big advantage for some students.

Based on the adaptive assessment technology within the program, the questions adjust themselves according to the student's need, thus personalizing the instruction for each student. Students also receive immediate feedback each time they answer a question. The software also is very appropriate for implementation of Tier 2 and Tier 3 RTI interventions. Teachers are able to select specific topics they want the student to work on, track the student's progress, and generate specific reports. Study Island creates a specified RTI report so that teachers can view student progress on a specific topic.

The PLATO Curriculum

Another technique that will characterize 21st-century classrooms is e-learning, where teachers will facilitate learning via technology and the entire lesson is presented by the computer (Davis, 2010b). Online learning is often a rigorous environment where students are connecting and communicating, often on a deeper level than in the classroom. *PLATO* Learning offers an extensive product line of technology-based teaching tools from online assessment tools to extended-day learning solutions for elementary and secondary students. Further, for middle and high school students, PLATO offers a version of e-learning with the entire core curriculums online.

Using this curriculum, students work through content at their own pace, on their own time. The courses in PLATO are semester long, and initial assessments place students in the course content that they need. Courses are aligned with state standards but can be customized by school districts or by individual teachers. PLATO, like other software-based instruction, offers teacher generated reports that detail student progress.

Courses offered by PLATO include online and offline activities with end-of-course assessments to show completion and mastery. Although the courses are self-paced, students are given multiple resources to ensure success, including a teacher's guide, a scope and sequence, instructional pacing, copies of all tests with grading keys, and rubrics.

Uses of Software-Based Instruction

We decided to include a brief description of these programs only to demonstrate that comprehensive curricula such as these now exist and are being increasingly used in schools. In particular, some are created to be basically supplemental, such as Study Island, whereas others, such as SuccessMaker and PLATO, are designed to replace whole courses within the curriculum. Increased use of these curricula will drastically impact schools, as more and more students are receiving their instruction in a one-on-one, computer-software-to-student format. This approach to mastering the curriculum truly represents freedom to learn anytime and anywhere. In that environment, teachers will be facilitators of learning (i.e., assisting students with problems the students encounter in the software-based instruction, or helping refocus students when they get off task) but not deliverers of knowledge (i.e., a traditional lecture). Clearly, increased use of this teaching paradigm will impact classrooms fairly drastically, and one may well ask, what happens to learning in that modern instructional environment?

THE LEARNING REVOLUTION

Coupled with the teaching revolution is a revolution in learning, and given these newly evolving instructional technologies, we might well ask, what happens to learning in the modern classroom? Of course, that question has resulted already in extensive discussions that could fill many volumes, and it cannot be addressed completely in this context. However, two major points are critical at this juncture.

First, research has shown that instruction using many of these tools results in increased engagement of students with the content and thus in increased understanding of that content (Ash, 2010; Davis, 2010b; Elder-Hinshaw et al., 2006; Richardson, 2010; Salend, 2009). In short, students do learn, and learn well, in computerized or web-based learning environments, which is why most universities are rushing to provide online university courses in virtually every subject.

> *Research has shown that instruction using many of these tools results in increased engagement of students with the content and thus in increased understanding of that content.*

Next, and perhaps most important, these technology tools are changing the form of not only teaching but also learning (Kay, 2010; Wilmarth, 2010). Whereas traditional instruction was driven by the teacher and based mainly on textbooks, lecture or discussion presentations, or videos and video-based discussions, today's teaching tools allow for students to direct their own learning process to a much higher degree. These modern teaching tools allow both students and teachers the exciting option of jointly creating knowledge and then publishing that knowledge to the world. It is not an overstatement to suggest that these tools are changing the very fabric of the traditional teaching/learning process. Again, this correlates well with several of the imaginings in the preface.

> *Today's teaching tools are changing the very fabric of the traditional teaching/learning process.*

For example, when teachers assign groups of students the option of creating a wiki on a local history item from the community, and then evaluate that wiki for accuracy, students are creating knowledge in a collaborative project and making that knowledge available worldwide. That is a very exciting option for many students. As schools evolve over the next few decades, many educators see a curriculum driven by student interest and creativity (Wilmarth, 2010), and we must note that student's heightened interest in completing such projects often has wonderful results in terms of higher student engagement, increased student mastery of knowledge, and reduction of inappropriate behaviors.

Further, the idea of a curriculum driven by and for student interest is one of the imaginings noted in the Introduction. Much more has been presented by others on how technologies might turn the curricular into a more individualistic, student-driven curricula (Jacobs, 2010; Wilmarth, 2010), and again this will be a revolution in the teaching/learning process. However, when coupled with both the RTI initiative and the concept of differentiated instruction, the possibilities of these technology innovations are staggering.

CONCLUSIONS

Given the nature of this changing field, it seems nearly impossible to write a chapter on how technology is impacting classrooms. Each new application, hardware, software, or teaching tool introduces many new instructional options, and trying to detail every possible technology tool a teacher might use is an insurmountable task. Many tools that are becoming quite common in classrooms are not discussed herein (e.g., PowerPoints, voice synthesizers, spell-checkers, grammar checkers, and a vast array of software programs), even though they are currently impacting instruction in classrooms around the country (Cote, 2007; Lange, Mulhern, & Wylie, 2009; Salend, 2009).

Still, our purpose was to present some of the technologies that are only beginning to be implemented to portray the sheer magnitude of the impact of technology over the next decade. Our goal is not to overwhelm teachers, to inundate them with new applications that they must learn, or to leave them feeling helpless. Rather, our goal is to introduce teachers to these tools and suggest some of the possibilities that are in our immediate future. Our curricula will certainly change, as the very teaching/learning process is redefined based on these emerging innovations (Kay, 2010; Wilmarth, 2010).

Another goal is to show the interaction of the technology applications with the ongoing RTI initiative across the nation. As schools move toward full RTI implementation in the basic skills of reading and mathematics, as well as for behavioral problems, technology is likely to play an increasing roll (Stewart et al., 2007). Again, the whole is greater than the sum of the parts when looking at RTI and technology, working in tandem to engage students and increase academic success.

Further, these technologies are fostering, and will continue to foster, an increase in the amount of differentiation teachers are able to perform in their classrooms. Webquests, blogs, podcasts, tweets—these tools motivate and engage students, making it possible for teachers to tailor each lesson to the individual needs of learners. It is vital that our students receive the best instruction possible, and embracing these technologies represent best instructional practice today (Ash, 2010; Kay, 2010; Manzo, 2010b; Partnership for 21st Century Skills, 2007, 2009a; Salend, 2009).

Teachers must realize that the students in their classrooms are already connected to this digital world, and they long for connectivity in every facet of their day. It is the job of the teacher to train these students in appropriate uses of these technologies and to help students see how this revolution in technology can impact their learning throughout their lives. As society continues to advocate 21st-century learning, it is vital that teachers embrace 21st-century tools without fear or hesitation (Gross & Spurka, 2010; Kay, 2010). This is not only the representation of several of the imaginings with which we began; this is the future of learning and the future of knowledge, for those whom we now teach.

3 The New Differentiated Instruction

Changing the Way Teachers Teach!

THE EVOLUTION OF DIFFERENTIATED INSTRUCTION

This chapter title is intentionally provocative to show the types of instructional change that we believe is coming to our classrooms! We realize that the whole-group lesson plan based on the instructional phases of a lesson as presented in Box 3.1 has been an icon in education for nearly fifty years, but we likewise believe that this lesson plan may have outlived its usefulness. Of course, teachers may well ask, "How can instruction be managed if not instruction directed at the whole class?"

Box 3.1   **Traditional Whole-Group Lesson Plan**

Introduction (hook-up activities; essential questions; brief high-interest activities)

Teacher-Led Instruction (model problems on the dry-erase board; general discussion of events in linear time)

Teacher-Guided Practice (students complete problems as the teacher scans or walks around the room helping students with difficulties)

Independent Practice (having students complete a series of problems or answer a series of questions alone either as classwork or homework)

Check and Reteach (assess understanding in some form; perhaps a few quiz questions, and reteach points students didn't get)

We believe that differentiated instruction, when coupled with the other innovations described in this text, will soon lead to a rather drastic decrease in whole-class instruction, if not an end to whole-class instructional lesson planning altogether (Bender, 2009a; Bender & Waller, 2011). Further, we believe the time has come for this type of lesson planning to end, in favor of differentiated instruction. Of course, this is already taking place in many classrooms and many schools, and is certainly likely to continue, given the other innovations such as RTI and increasing use of technologies for instruction. Still, by stating this so forcefully, we realize that we are moving beyond what Dr. Carol Tomlinson, the originator of the differentiated instructional concept, has advocated; indeed, she recently wrote that differentiation should not lead to the wholesale abandonment of whole-class instruction (Tomlinson, 2010). However, we respectfully disagree and believe that whole-class instruction should and must be swept aside as an instructional idea whose time has come and gone. To make that argument, we present a discussion of how differentiated instruction, as a concept, has both transformed our instructional models and been transformed by current classroom practices and ongoing research. We begin by a discussion of what differentiation was originally.

Origins of Differentiated Instruction

Differentiated instruction was first defined and described by Tomlinson over a decade ago (1999) as a way to provide an increased set of different instructional activities to address the increasingly diverse learning needs of students in today's classrooms. From this perspective, provision of a single set of educational activities was no longer considered sufficient to provide adequate learning experiences for all students, since the academic diversity of the students in most general education classes was then, as it is today, much greater than in previous years. Also, insights into the varied learning styles of these highly diverse students allowed teachers to plan specific instructional tactics based on the varied learning styles of the students (Bender, 2008; Gregory & Kuzmich, 2005; Marzano, 2010a, 2010b; Smutny & Von Fremd, 2010).

> *The recent RTI initiative has restructured elementary reading and has begun to restructure middle and high school instruction as well.*

Initially, Tomlinson developed the differentiated instruction concept based on several different areas of instructional theory, including a primary emphasis on multiple intelligences theory (Gardner, 1983, 2006; Moran, Kornhaber, & Gardner, 2006) and a lesser emphasis on the more recent brain-compatible instruction literature (Caine & Caine, 2006; Sousa, 2005, 2009; Tate, 2005). To practice differentiated instruction, teachers had to know the learners in the class, not only understanding a student's multiple intelligences strengths but also developing a wide array of instructional activities and procedures that were tailored to meet the needs of each individual student (Bender & Waller, 2011; Gregory, 2008). In short, the wider academic diversity in classrooms required a wider array of learning activities to reach each learner, and the teacher's job was to design and provide a set of different learning activities based on the individual needs of the students.

Teaching Content, Process, and Product

In the development of differentiated instruction, Tomlinson (1999) identified three possible ways to modify instruction to develop differentiated lesson activities; these included variations in the content, the instructional process, and the student products produced as a result of their learning. Over the last decade, these have become the foundation for most differentiation efforts (Bender, 2008; Smutny & Von Fremd, 2010).

Originally, variations in content, such as the amount of content presented to various students, were considered critical to successful differentiation. Teachers had options concerning how much content was presented, as well as the depth of presentation of that content. That is, teachers could modify content for presentation to the students based on the learning styles of the students in the class, and in that modification process, some content might be emphasized more than other material for certain groups of students (Bender, 2008; Smutny & Von Fremd, 2010; Tomlinson, 1999).

In differentiation based on the learning process, the instructional activities might be varied based on the process students must go through to master the content. For example, students with a strength in visual/spatial learning might be assigned to draw pictures of critical battles or events in a history lesson on the American Revolution (e.g., pictures of Valley Forge showing the freezing snow, and the suffering that almost wiped out the Patriot Army). Others with linguistic strengths might be required to delineate, in outline form, the reasons for the Revolution (taxation without representation, governmental policies that were anticommerce in the colonies, etc.). Students who seem to learn best through physical activity might be assigned to act out one of the major battles of the Revolution. In these examples, the learning process is varied, though the overall content remains the same. Also, as these examples indicate, such differentiation could be based on the multiple intelligences strengths of each student (Sternberg, 2006).

> *The learning process is varied, though the overall content remains the same.*

Finally, variations in the learning product provide another venue for differentiated instruction in the class (Smutny & Von Fremd, 2010; Tomlinson, 1999). Again, the learning styles and strengths of the students in the class should help determine what types of products the teacher should accept as appropriate demonstrations of learning. In the differentiated classroom, it is very appropriate for a given instructional unit to offer a choice of three or four different types of culminating projects. Some students may choose art projects that demonstrate a deep understanding of the content, whereas others may develop mini-dramas that exemplify the content under study. Web-based research projects and development of multimedia presentations all represent legitimate products that can demonstrate knowledge of the subject content.

Over the years, various proponents of differentiated instruction have recommended that a wider array of instructional activities be included in the curriculum across the age span (Bender, 2008; Connor & Lagares, 2007; Gregory, 2008), and research has indicated that more modifications within the curriculum does result in higher student engagement, increased achievement, and fewer behavior problems among high school students (Lee, Wehmeyer, Soukup, & Palmer, 2010; Tomlinson, 2010). Thus, differentiation has been strongly recommended over the last decade, as a more individualized instructional emphasis than traditional whole-group instruction (Bender, 2008).

> *The wider academic diversity in today's classrooms requires a wider array of learning activities, and the teacher's job in today's classrooms is to design and provide that set of learning activities, based on the individual needs of the students.*

The New Differentiation: Modification of the Concept

With that brief discussion in mind, there are several notable shifts in recent descriptions of differentiated instruction; taken together, these modifications of the original idea are leading toward a "new" differentiation, a modernized and upgraded form of the differentiation concept. In fact, yesterday's discussions of differentiated instruction do not really capture the importance of this concept, nor do they suggest the real potential for this construct to impact classroom instruction (Bender, 2008; Bender & Waller, 2011; Tomlinson, 2010; Tomlinson, Brimijoin, & Narvaez, 2008). The identification and description of the several ways that the differentiated instruction concept has morphed in recent years demonstrates the significance of this change.

First, the multiple intelligences basis for differentiation has been largely de-emphasized in recent work on differentiation. In the early literature on differentiated instruction (Tomlinson, 1999), there was a heavy emphasis on the theory of multiple intelligences, as developed by Dr. Howard Gardner (Gardner, 1983, 2006; Moran et al., 2006). Teachers were encouraged to form educational groups for differentiated activities based on similar multiple intelligences strengths to such a degree that some in education initially perceived differentiated instruction as merely the classroom description of the multiple intelligences construct, and many of the early books on differentiation practice were heavily based in that construct at that time (Gregory, 2008; Gregory & Kuzmich, 2005).

However, the concept of differentiation has now moved beyond the multiple intelligences construct, and in many recent discussions of differentiation, the multiple intelligences theory is not even mentioned (Bender & Waller, 2011; Tomlinson, 2010; Tomlinson et al., 2008; Tomlinson & McTighe, 2006). Instead, recent discussions of differentiation have shifted to emphasize a broader array of learning styles and preferences, coupled with the more solidly founded research on actual brain functioning during learning tasks (Tomlinson, 2010; Tomlinson et al., 2008; Tomlinson & McTighe, 2006). Unlike the multiple intelligences theory, a theory that never received widespread research support, the growing literature on brain functioning is solidly based on research in the neurosciences (Sousa, 2005, 2009, 2010; Tate, 2005) and thus provides a stronger research base for differentiation than multiple intelligences theory.

Next, the three areas in which differentiation were recommended have shifted somewhat. As stated already, the initial differentiation concept emphasized differentiation in content, learning processes, and the learning products produced by the students. Today, there is considerably less emphasis on modifying the learning content and more emphasis on the learning process and variations in the learning products (Tomlinson, 2010; Tomlinson et al., 2008; Tomlinson & McTighe, 2006). This shift in emphasis is logical since today, much more so than in the late 1990s, state educational standards in most cases dictate the instructional content. Tomlinson (2010) has responded to this by indicating that while teachers can't vary the content a great deal, they can and should differentiate how students gain access to key educational content.

Third, over the last decade, the impact of differentiated instruction has been demonstrated by actual increases in student achievement in several instances (Lee et al., 2010; Tomlinson et al., 2008). Initially, differentiated instruction was merely a theory that, it was suggested, might engage students more in learning the content as teachers addressed their learning strengths, but little evidence for the actual efficacy of differentiation was presented. In contrast, there have recently been several reports of improvements in academic performance resulting from increased differentiation. In fact, in a recent book, Tomlinson and her coauthors demonstrated the efficacy of differentiated instruction in terms of improved academic scores and increased number of students passing statewide achievement assessments (Tomlinson et al., 2008). While not evidence from a controlled scientific study, this school-based evidence for efficacy of differentiation is nevertheless both new and impressive.

In a controlled research study, Lee, Wehmeyer, Soukup, and Palmer (2010) showed that modifications of curricular presentation did result in improved academic achievement and fewer behavior problems. Of course, research evidence for efficacy of differentiated instruction is still quite limited, but basing discussions of differentiation on research efficacy is a critical and important step, and the available evidence does suggest the efficacy of moving toward more differentiated instruction (Lee et al., 2010; Tomlinson, 2010; Tomlinson et al., 2008).

Fourth, educators across the country have now recognized that differentiation is much more than merely an educational fad; rather, differentiation represents a significant change in instructional practice. A move toward differentiation at the school level involves more than a workshop or two for the faculty; rather, such a shift will necessitate an ongoing modification of instructional belief systems as well as instructional practices. For this reason, differentiated instruction has been called a second-order change in education (Tomlinson et al., 2008).

First-order changes in educational procedures can be incremental, usually don't involve changes in fundamental beliefs, and may be accomplished by several one-time workshops with the faculty. In contrast, a second-order change will require a drastic departure from the status quo. Thus, second-order change is much more invasive and will necessitate a dramatic departure from current beliefs and instructional practices. Tomlinson and her coauthors have argued that differentiation must be a second-order change in the very fabric of instruction to really impact student achievement (Tomlinson et al., 2008), and the nation seems to be responding to this call for intensive differentiation. This was shown quite clearly when state after state built statewide RTI policies on the foundation of differentiated instruction as the exemplar of appropriate Tier 1 instruction. Most statewide RTI plans specifically mentioned differentiated instruction by name (Berkeley et al., 2009) as the most appropriate basis for RTI. Again, differentiation is not an educational fad but rather represents a substantive change in how teachers teach; it is a revolution in education. The very title of Tomlinson's recent book clearly states the revolutionary nature of the implementation of differentiated instruction (Tomlinson et al., 2008).

> *Differentiation is not an educational fad but rather a substantive change in how teachers teach; it is a revolution in education.*

Finally, as technology innovations such as those described in Chapter 2 are increasingly incorporated into classroom instruction, it is likely that technology itself may begin to drive our moves toward differentiation. We should point out that many of the social-networking technologies, interactive instructional technologies, and computerized instructional programs used today did not even exist when Tomlinson did her initial work on differentiated instruction (1999), and clearly technology can drastically increase the time that individual students receive specific instruction targeted directly toward their individual learning needs. Thus, technology is changing the face of the differentiated instruction concept, and it is almost impossible to discuss one without the other.

In fact, this interactive synthesis forms the core principle of this book, namely, that technology, RTI, and differentiated instruction are mutually supporting, and that the change to come from this interactive synthesis is far more significant than the change that either of these factors would lead to alone.

In an extreme example, it is hard to imagine any classroom that could be more highly differentiated than a class in which each student was working on computer-based software or with an online, web-based instructional program at exactly his or her academic level for every subject in the curricula. Not only does such application of technology lead to the extreme differentiation of completely independent and individualized instruction; it likewise fosters daily or weekly progress monitoring for all students, thus complimenting the school's RTI efforts. As indicated in the previous chapter, many of the technologies emerging today are only now being incorporated into our instructional practices, but it is hard to even imagine the options for differentiated instruction that technology will soon provide.

> Not only does application of technology lead to the extreme differentiation of completely independent and individual instruction; it likewise fosters daily or weekly progress monitoring for all students, thus complimenting the school's RTI efforts.

Given these shifts in emphasis, it seems appropriate to suggest that differentiation today represents a new, and somewhat different, concept from differentiation concept of 1999 (Tomlinson, 1999). Further, the new differentiation provides the critical backdrop for the other innovations such as RTI and technology-based instruction for the 21st century. In describing this new differentiation, we will examine the ongoing emphasis on learning preferences as well as the ever-growing brain-compatible instructional emphasis that undergirds differentiated instruction. Then a classroom-based model of differentiated instruction will be described that can easily be applied across the grade levels. The ultimate impact of this concept will be either a significant decrease in or the ultimate demise of whole class lesson planning and whole-class instruction.

However, it is critical to point out that differentiated instruction is also the foundation on which both the new instructional technologies and the RTI initiative, as described in Chapter 1, are based. Because technology-based instruction is almost always individual instruction, it meets the criteria for increased differentiation of instructional activities. Further, general education teachers today have an absolute responsibility to provide differentiated instruction as the Tier 1 basis for the higher intervention tiers in the RTI process. In today's schools, tiered instruction for RTI must be founded on differentiated instruction within the general education class (Bender, 2009a). It is because of this synthesis of technology and RTI that we must closely examine differentiated instruction as the instructional model for 21st-century schools.

> *General education teachers today have an absolute responsibility to provide differentiated instruction as the Tier 1 basis for the higher intervention tiers in the RTI process.*

LEARNING STYLES AND THE NEW DIFFERENTIATION

As mentioned previously, the emphasis on multiple intelligences has decreased in the literature on differentiation, while researchers are increasingly discussing the broader concept of diverse learning styles as the basis for forming differentiated groups of students for different activities within the class (Marzano, 2010a, 2010b; Silver & Perini; 2010; Sternberg, 2006; Tomlinson, 2010; Tomlinson et al., 2008). A variety of instructional activities used today in classrooms result from consideration of students' varied learning styles. For example, in many classrooms today, as well as in many textbooks, one can frequently find specific instructional recommendations for the "spatial" learner, or the "bodily kinesthetic" learner.

> *In many classrooms today, as well as in many textbooks, one can frequently find specific instructional recommendations based on learning styles, such as recommendations for the "spatial" learner, or the "bodily kinesthetic" learner.*

Spatial thinkers often seem to understand content more quickly when a diagram is presented to illustrate the concept. Thus, the concrete, representational, abstract instructional approach is frequently used in which mathematics calculations, even in the middle and upper elementary grades, might be illustrated with physical manipulatives (the concrete emphasis) or tally marks (the representational emphasis using groups of tally marks as a representation of a two-digit multiplication problem) prior to moving to doing mathematics problems abstractly (Bender, 2009b). As another example, the student with a strength in spatial learning might be shown how to "take notes" in the form of semantic webs and then to use those to help develop outline notes on the course content. This skill will help that student over the long term in all of his or her academic work.

Some students seem to grasp the content only when movement is involved. These are typically referred to as *bodily kinesthetic learners*, and they should be taught in a way that allows them to represent and understand the content through movement. For example, middle- and upper-grade teachers today are teaching about circulation of the blood through the heart by presenting a four-chamber diagram of the heart on the floor and having the students move through the chambers in the order of flowing blood, including leaving the heart to go to the lungs and retrieve oxygen, returning to the heart, and then leaving again to take oxygen to the body. Students who are bodily kinesthetic learners will master that type of content more quickly when "moving through" it than when studying it from the text, from a video, or from an overhead (Gregory, 2008).

No definitive list of learning styles exists, because many different proponents of this instructional approach recommend different terms. Learning styles can range from light sensitivity, to memory patterns, to thought processes, even to many of the multiple intelligences. However, a number of learning styles have been discussed in this literature more so than some of the others, and some of the commonly recognized learning styles are presented in Box 3.2.

Box 3.2 **Learning Style Instructional Ideas for Teaching About the New Deal**

Analytic/Linguistic Learners: These students learn best linguistically and are very adept at creating outlines of events or organizing content in other ways. Have some students with a linguistic strength work together to develop an outline of the period from 1928 through 1940, including the crash of 1929, the election of Roosevelt, and his New Deal legislation. Use that outline as a teaching tool throughout the unit.

Auditory Learners: Some students master material better when they hear it than when they see it, and these may be considered auditory learners. Rather than read about the New Deal, these students might need to listen to one of Roosevelt's "fireside chats" from that time period.

Visual Learners: This is generally the same group that some may refer to as *spatial learners*. They will need to visualize history, and multimedia presentations of Roosevelt and the Congress enacting New Deal legislation will be helpful for this group, as will graphic organizers of that legislation.

Interpersonal: These students need to synthesize information together. Thus, they, like the auditory learners, should listen to one of Roosevelt's fireside chats and discuss the impact that his speech might have had on a nation where 25 percent of the population was unemployed.

(Continued)

(Box 3.2 Continued)

Global Thinkers: Global thinkers need to see the whole picture and learn specific factual content from that broader perspective. These students will need to begin with a completed timeline that presents a clear picture of the whole period, including the market crash of 1929, the New Deal, and the end of the Depression that took place because of the industrial buildup of the Lend-Lease programs and World War II.

Sequential Thinkers: These are the opposite of global thinkers. These students will need to study these historical events in highly defined sequential order, finding the cause for subsequent events within previous events. These students should "build" a timeline of events as they study each historical event during this period, rather than begin with a completed timeline.

Bodily Kinesthetic and *Interpersonal:* Bodily kinesthetic learners need to experience or move through the content, and interpersonal learners need to work with others to master content. Often these two groups can work together, as in this example. The teacher might select one main scene from the social studies text, from the Internet, or from various software programs. These students can then review that and develop a one-act play about that event, which can be presented to the class later in the unit.

Mathematical: These students seem to want to quantify knowledge in some form and understand best when such quantification is possible. Using a list of New Deal legislation, compute how many persons were provided jobs resulting from various programs (e.g., Civilian Conservation Corps, farm legislation).

Musical: Students with a musical talent will master more content when some is presented musically or in a rhymetic fashion. Teachers might have these students create a chant, a rap, or a song to describe the New Deal, and possibly even relate it to the recession of 2007–2009.

Instruction based on learning styles involves planning lessons that present opportunities for various types of activities that address each of the main learning style areas (Gregory, 2008; Smutny & Von Fremd, 2010; Tate, 2005; Tomlinson & McTighe, 2006). Various proponents have suggested that increasing the instructional activities with this focus will increase academic engagement of many students, and thus increase learning, and there seems to be some evidence for that (Moran et al., 2006; Silver & Perini, 2010; Sternberg, 2006; Tomlinson et al., 2008). However, questions have been raised based on the lack of widespread research basis for the learning styles instructional approach (Silver & Perini, 2010; Sousa, 2010), and some caution is in order when considering use of this instructional approach.

> *Instruction based on learning styles involves planning lessons that present opportunities for various types of activities that address each of the main learning style areas.*

However, the concept of differentiating instruction to address learning styles has highlighted several points on which educators generally do agree (Bender, 2008; Moran et al., 2006; Silver & Perini, 2010). First, students learn differently, and this knowledge allows teachers to create more varied instructional activities for teaching the class content (Silver & Perini, 2010; Sternberg, 2006). Also, proponents of differentiated instruction assert that expanding the range of educational activities in the classroom is likely to enhance the on-task time of many students, some of whom may have been somewhat marginalized previously by their nonlinguistic learning style in classrooms where most activities were linguistic in nature. Nonlinguistic teaching, at the very least, tends to be rather different from paper-and-pencil workshops, and educators agree that instructional novelty increases attention and thereby academic performance (Silver & Perini, 2010; Sousa, 2005).

For these reasons, many practitioners have advocated use of various learning styles approaches for educational planning purposes, even though the supporting research is somewhat underdeveloped at present (Bender, 2008, 2009b; Gregory & Kuzmich, 2005; Moran et al., 2006; Silver & Perini, 2010; Smutny & Von Fremd, 2010; Sousa, 2010; Sternberg, 2006; Tate, 2005; Tomlinson et al., 2008).

> *Expanding the range of educational activities in the classroom is likely to enhance on-task time, because instructional novelty seems to increase attention and thereby academic performance.*

BRAIN-COMPATIBLE RESEARCH AND THE NEW DIFFERENTIATION

How Brains Learn

A more solid research base for differentiated instruction than learning styles is the growing body of research on how brains function during the learning process (Caine & Caine, 2006; Doidge, 2007; King & Gurian, 2006; Merzenich, 2001; Merzenich, Tallal, Peterson, Miller, & Jenkins, 1999; Sousa, 2005, 2009, 2010; Tate, 2005; Tomlinson, 2010). Much of this research stems from the development of the functional magnetic resonance imaging techniques, or fMRI (Doidge, 2007; Merzenich, 2001; Merzenich et al., 1999; Sousa, 2005). An fMRI is a nonradiological brain-scanning technique, based on the more familiar MRI technology, that has allowed scientists to study the functioning of human brains while the subjects concentrated on different types of learning tasks (Caine & Caine, 2006; Sousa, 2005).

> *A more solid research base for differentiated instruction than learning styles is the growing body of research on how brains function during the learning process.*

Specifically, the fMRI measures the brain's use of oxygen and sugar during the thinking process, and from that information, psychologists have determined very precisely which brain areas are most active during various types of cognitive tasks (Sousa, 2005). The more those two nutrients are consumed in that specific brain area, the more active it is in the learning process. In short, this brain-imaging technique can show, with high precision, the degree to which specific areas of the brain are optimally engaged in learning. We now know that language involves activation of certain brain areas, while music or chanting stimulates other areas, and movement still others. Further combining these three activities stimulates all of those areas, making retention of any material studied in that activity more likely. Of course, in the vast majority of cognitive tasks, multiple brain areas are involved, but one general guideline has been documented: The more brain regions that are actively involved during a learning task, the more likely long-term learning becomes.

> *The more brain areas that are actively involved in a task, the more likely that long-term learning results.*

However, the power of the fMRI technology has shown us much more than merely regional brain activity. We have now begun to understand learning at the cellular level. Specifically, neurons are the brain cells associated with learning and thinking, and neurons communicate with each other through tentacles at their endpoint; those tentacles are called *dendrites* (Sousa, 2005). Dendrites are a part of every neuron that branch out specifically to communicate with other neurons, and as dendrites communicate with other brain cells nearby, they develop a consistent set of neuron to neuron connections that may be thought of as a set of predictable cellular communication connections that represents "learning." When dendritic connections are extensive enough and repeated often enough, learning takes place. Thus, learning can be defined as neurons communicating with each other in a predictable way that has been established over repeated practice and is associated with particular stimuli in the environment.

Dendrites function, in one sense, as electrical switches that "fire" by producing a small measurable charge of electricity. However, neurons do not generally touch each other, so the electric signal from neuron to neuron is transmitted across the space between the two cells when one cell releases a chemical called a neurotransmitter that then interacts with the next neuron (Bender, 2008; Sousa, 2005). However, the critical aspect for learning involves the predictable set of neurons firing together that become associated with a particular thought or concept.

One phrase that is popular in much of the literature on brain functioning sums up this concept of dendritic connections between brain cells: "Cells that fire together, wire together" (Doidge, 2007). The phrase means that as cells repeatedly activate each other through these dendritic connections, that set of cells is more likely to fire together in the future—thus learning takes place.

> *Learning can be defined as neurons communicating with each other in a predictable way that has been established over repeated practice and is associated with particular stimuli in the environment.*

Of course, this is a very elementary level of understanding of cell-to-cell interactions in the brain, and no single chapter on differentiation can summarize the complexity of these interactions or the instructional insights that have stemmed from this growing body of brain research. A few research-based conclusions on sex-specific brain functioning are presented in Box 3.3, just to show the types of insights emerging from this literature and how this work might impact class instruction. Further, the next section examines in a general way the instructional implications of this literature to date.

Box 3.3   Gender Differences That Impact Learning

Visual system differences: Young girls and young boys have several differences in their visual system. Specifically, the visual system of males tends to rely more heavily on Type M ganglion cells, which are the visual cells that detect movement. In contrast, females generally have more Type P ganglion cells that are more sensitive to color variety. As a result, males may rely more on moving objects to master content, whereas females tend to focus more on color, picture detail, and other color-based sensory information. Of course, novel visual material (variations in color coded material or movement representing the content) is quite effective in teaching, but these techniques are likely to be differentially effective for males and females.

(Continued)

(Box 3.3 Continued)

Cross-talk between brain hemispheres: Females are probably better at multitasking than males because structural differences in females' brains generate more cross-talk between the brain hemispheres. Males' brains, on the other hand, tend to lateralize and compartmentalize brain activity much more so that females. Thus, females tend to pay attention to more information on more subjects at any given time, whereas males tend to concentrate best when they follow specific steps while focusing on a single task.

Male's natural aggression: Males are more naturally aggressive and competitive than females, and this is based, in part, on brain functioning. For this reason, males gravitate toward aggressive tasks whereas females gravitate toward competitive learning activities. Males also tend toward greater impulsivity, which can lead to increased aggression. Also, they have less desire than females to comply with instructions or to please others, including the teacher. This suggests engagement of males may be enhanced by competitive gaming simulation activities focused on the learning content, whereas females might do better with cooperative learning tasks. Of course, teachers should make certain that all students are exposed to some degree to both.

Frontal lobe differences: In one area, female brains develop a bit more quickly than male brains. The prefrontal cortex in females develops more quickly, and that area is associated with reasoning and efficient decision making, as well as reading and word production. This developmental difference may account for the fact that females tend to be slightly less impulsive than males in the primary grades.

Verbal/spatial brain differences: Some research suggests that the brains of young males have more cortical areas dedicated to spatial-mechanical functioning than females (King & Gurian, 2006). This difference may play a role in the higher mathematics achievement, on average, among boys. In contrast, young females' brains generally have greater cortical emphasis on verbal-emotive processing. This shows up in classroom behavior because females use more words on average than males do, and females tend to think more verbally in the primary and elementary grades.

Neural rest states: Males' brains lapse into what neurologists refer to as a *neural rest state* more frequently than young females (King & Gurian, 2006). This may lead to males being more likely to "zone out" in class. Some boys may attempt to arrest these natural rest states by engaging in self-stimulation activities, such as moving around the class, playing, or engaging others in conversation. In short, when the male brain gets bored, some of the brain functioning shuts down, which negates the possibility of effective learning. However, when the female brain gets bored, more of the brain functioning remains active, and thus, even when a young girl is bored, she is more likely to retain the ability to participate in relatively passive instructional activities in class such as taking notes, or listening. Males are much less likely to participate in such passive activities.

*Information adapted from King and Gurian (2006) and Sousa (2005, 2010).

What Does This Brain Research Suggest for Teaching?

Educators today see a plethora of instructional tactics and recommendations that stem from this body of research (Bender, 2008; Gregory, 2008; Sousa, 2005, 2010; Tate, 2005), and these varied instructional tactics often undergird differentiated instruction. For example, we now have evidence that intensive instruction can and does impact brain activity directly (Simos et al., 2007), and this ongoing research is suggestive of specific types of instructional activities that more actively involve the entire brain.

Activities that are highly novel offer students some choices in what they do, involve multiple brain regions, and involve tactics keyed to various learning styles or activities that encourage the student to have fun and enjoy the learning activity—all are strongly supported by this growing body of research (Bender, 2008). In fact, not only have instructional suggestions arisen from this body of research (Gregory, 2008; Sousa, 2005, 2009, 2010; Tate, 2005); there are now also a number of technology-based curricular programs based on this exciting, emerging knowledge of how brains function, such as the Fast ForWord reading curricula (Doidge, 2007).

The movement example presented earlier, dealing with blood circulation through the human heart, would involve multiple brain regions and would thus be a recommended activity among proponents of brain-compatible teaching. Further, the use of songs, chants, and rhythms to represent content is likewise now recommended across the grade levels (Bender, 2008; Tate, 2005). Teachers have long realized that having students verbally rehearse the letters of the alphabet in sequential order will activate many brain cells and lead to learning. However, having students "sing" the alphabet, as have many primary teachers over the years, activates many more brain regions, including those areas associated with letter sounds and memory for letter shapes as memory for the tune, musical understanding, and a variety of other brain areas. This results in higher-impact learning of that content.

While primary teachers have been using songs and chants for years, we now realize that songs, chants, and rhythms are very powerful teaching techniques across the grade levels (Bender, 2009b). Proponents of differentiation are recommending this technique, since so many brain areas become involved with the content (Tate, 2005), and mixing a movement with a song or chant that summarizes the essence of the content is likewise recommended (Bender, 2009b; Tate, 2005). Here is a rhythmic chant, recently developed by some teachers in a workshop in Pennsylvania, that uses a military marching cadence in which the "Sergeant" shouts the term and the others reply with the definition as they march in place.

Alliteration	*//*	*repetition of initial sound.*
Assonance	*//*	*repetition of middle sound.*
Anaphora	*//*	*repetition of the starting word.*
Stanza	*//*	*Separate grouping of the lines.*
Rhyme Scheme	*//*	*The way rhyming words are arranged.*
What's This	*//*	*This is how poetry is made!*

Clearly, this chant can teach content from the upper grade levels, and using chants such as this across the grade levels makes memorization of those definitions a bit more interesting, as more brain areas are involved in learning that content. For that reasons, we recommend that teachers across all grade levels not let an instructional period go by without using a song or chant in every instructional unit to teach the critical elements of the instructional content for that unit (Bender, 2008)!

> *Teachers should not let a single instructional period go by without a song/ rhythm/chant to teach the critical elements of the instructional content for that unit!*

However, using songs, chants, and raps is not a never-ending process of creation, nor should a different song or chant be used every day. Rather, the critical and most important content from an instructional unit should be summed up in eight to sixteen lines and then put into a song or rhythm. That *same* song, rap, rhythm, or chant should then be repeated each day during the instructional unit, since daily repetition of that essential content is not only fun but also increases the students' memory for that content. Such use of these teaching ideas is quite likely to lead to long-term learning.

While understanding the intricacies of brain or neuron functioning is not our goal in this context, teachers should be aware of this research as the basis for brain-compatible instruction and differentiated instruction.

Again, many instructional recommendations have been made for teachers based on this brain-compatible instruction research (Bender, 2008; Gregory, 2008; Sousa, 2005, 2009; Tate, 2005), and all of these cannot be summarized in this context. However, Box 3.4 presents some guidelines for teachers who wish to plan instructional activities that are brain friendly in various content areas across the grade levels.

Box 3.4   Brain-Compatible Teaching Tips

Write out the critical content. What are the big ideas to be taught? Teachers should identify that critical content, those big ideas, with and for the students. This should be limited to eight to twelve main points in any given unit of instruction. These may be terms, graphics, or concepts that students should learn for life. Those points will become the main content that is used to develop high-impact, brain-compatible instructional tactics.

Arrange these points in some logical order. What order can be imposed on those points? Perhaps a causal order will work, or a temporal order. Maybe some type of spatial relationship makes sense for the content. That ordering will aid students' memory for those main points. The teacher should then describe the basis for that order in some fashion (i.e., a picture representation, causal, time ordered).

Create a visual aide to represent that content. If possible, picture those ordered points in some type of graphic, chart, or multimedia computer-based presentation. Use novel instructional enhancements such as color coding, size-of-print differences, or movements to represent the content. Alternatively, teachers may use a small group of students in a differentiated teaching activity to create those representations.

Use humor. Share or have students develop a humorous story or poem on those main points if possible. If the teacher has a humorous idea about representing these big ideas, the teacher should jot the idea down and have a differentiated group of students develop it. Make certain that each important aspect of the content is covered, if possible.

Tie those big ideas to positive emotions, if possible. In many cases, a personal story or the experiences from the teacher or another member of the school or community will help focus students' attention on the big ideas. This will lead to long-term retention. Use positive emotional ties to the content whenever possible.

(Continued)

(Box 3.4 Continued)

Think of or create a song or chant that can be used for teaching those points. Is there a period piece of music, or a popular song, that represents a similar theme? Teachers should use students with a musical talent to put those main points into a song or chant. Many times a military cadence will work, if no one can think of an appropriate song.

Create a movement to represent those points. Develop a movement, or have a group of students develop a movement, that teaches the eight to twelve essential concepts. Where possible, couple that movement with the chant or song, and repeat that movement/song/chant activity daily throughout the unit.

*Ideas adapted from a variety of sources (Bender, 2008; Sousa, 2005, 2010; Tate, 2005).

EVIDENCE OF IMPACT OF DIFFERENTIATED AND BRAIN-COMPATIBLE INSTRUCTION

Some indicators of the impact of differentiated instruction and brain-compatible instruction have emerged in recent years (Caine & Caine, 2006; Doidge, 2007; King & Gurian, 2006; Lee et al., 2010; Merzenich, 2001; Silver & Perini, 2010; Sternberg, 2006; Tate, 2005; Tomlinson, 2010; Tomlinson et al., 2008). For example, as mentioned previously, Tomlinson and her coauthors (2008) presented evidence of academic improvement across the core subjects of reading, language arts, and mathematics in two schools that implemented differentiated instruction.

In another schoolwide implementation study, King and Gurian (2006) described a school in Colorado in which teachers noted a sharp achievement gap (a gap of 21 percent on the state reading text) between young males and young females. Males were falling behind females consistently in the reading curriculum, and the faculty became concerned and began to study the matter. They looked into the brain-compatible research on gender differences (see Box 3.3) and found that their reading curriculum might favor the brain-based learning styles of young girls more so than young boys. Further, they concluded that the reading curriculum itself might likewise favor young girls.

In particular, when students were presented with an array of reading materials, males and females chose different types of material (King & Gurian, 2006). Males chose to read topics with more conflict between characters and very clear role distinctions between heroes and villains. They often chose reading topics with a hint of danger and aggression, and stories that involve clear winners and losers, including reading material on topics such as NASCAR, football, atomic bombs, battles, or animals fighting (King & Gurain, 2006). In contrast, females tend to avoid reading material that represents high levels of overt conflict, preferring topics such as relationships, deep friendships, or fantasy material (e.g., such as mermaids and unicorns). Further, the teachers then investigated the stories in the basal reading curriculum and found that the stories that appealed to young girls' interests clearly outnumbered the stories that would appeal to boys.

> *Males frequently choose to read topics with clear role distinctions between heroes and villains, often reading topics with a hint of danger and aggression, and stories that involve clear winners and losers. In contrast, females tend to choose topics such as friendship or relationships.*

With this information in hand, the faculty collectively determined to supplement their reading curriculum with additional stories that were of more interest to males (King & Gurian, 2006). Also, having studied the differentiated instruction and brain-compatible instructional literature, teachers began to teach with more attention to novel stimuli, conflict, and movement-based instruction. As a result of these modifications, the school was able to close the reading achievement gap between young males and young females in only one year.

While clearly an anecdotal example from one school, this result nevertheless does indicate the potential for highly differentiated brain-compatible instruction to enhance academic achievement in one school (King & Gurian, 2006). Further, with mounting evidence in support of differentiated instruction based on brain-compatible instructional techniques, teachers should anticipate implementing more of these techniques in the immediate future.

> *When teachers began to teach with more attention to novel stimuli, conflict, and movement-based instruction, this Colorado school was able to close a reading achievement gap between males and females in one year.*

Conclusions About Brains and Learning

While brain research is ongoing, there are several conclusions that can be drawn from this research that impact how educators may wish to implement brain-compatible differentiated instructional activities in their classes. First, engaging our students' brains in active, deep thought on the content is critical for higher-level conceptual learning (Bender, 2008; Doidge, 2007; Merzenich, 2001; Merzenich et al., 1999; Sousa, 2010). While many different proponents have provided guidelines, the key is to engage students' brains with critical content in a fashion that stimulates maximum brain involvement. Teaching strategies and activities that engage brains in that fashion may be considered high-impact teaching tactics (see the examples in Box 3.3 and Box 3.4), since they are more likely to lead to long-term retention than traditional instructional techniques.

Next, active cognitive engagement with the critical content in an instructional unit is probably more critical than "content coverage" for overall mastery of the content. Therefore, the idea of "teaching less content, but teaching it more thoroughly" is a sound teaching principle across the public school grades. Of course, this holds implications for the standards-based instruction movement, which will be discussed in the next chapter. In short, we now know that teaching too much content is the rough equivalent of teaching nothing at all over the long term.

> *Teaching less content, but teaching it more thoroughly, is a sound teaching principle.*

Next, effective teaching involves creating exciting, innovative differentiated learning activities that will actively engage today's students with the learning content in a rich, meaningful, highly involved manner (Bender, 2008, 2009; Doidge, 2007; Sousa, 2010; Tomlinson & McTighe, 2006). Today's students expect and respond to nothing less than the stimulation they have grown used to in today's digital, media-rich, highly interactive world, and teachers must structure their instruction to approximate that modern world, to whatever degree possible. Thus, using brain-compatible teaching ideas, coupled with modern technologies to engage our students, is now critical (Davis, 2010b; Manzo, 2010a, 2010b). Teachers must create differentiated learning activities that emulate the high-tech world of our students, and on that basis, instruction is much more likely to be more effective (Bender, 2008; Connor & Lagares, 2007; Gregory, 2008; Lee et al., 2010; Manzo, 2010a, 2010b).

> *Today's students expect and respond to nothing less than the stimulation they have grown used to in today's digital, media-rich, highly interactive world, and teachers must structure their instruction to approximate that modern world.*

Next, to whatever degree possible, teachers should create "authentic" learning environments in which students actually "experience" the content, or produce the content, rather that merely read about it, discuss it, or study it. Interactive activities—such as creation of podcasts, Internet searches, and group projects based on web-based collaborative development tools such as Google Docs—are likely to enhance learning much more so than traditional "read, discuss, and test" instruction. Such "experiential learning" will result in deeper understanding and longer-term learning of the content in question (Moran et al., 2006; Sternberg, 2006).

DIFFERENTIATION THROUGH LEARNING CENTERS

At this point, teachers might well ask, "What does the new differentiation look like in a real classroom?" or "How exactly will differentiated instruction cause classrooms to look different?" The new differentiation can take many forms in the classroom, and many models of differentiated instruction have been presented over the years (Bender, 2009b; Gregory, 2008; Tomlinson, 1999, 2001, 2010). For example, Bender (2009b) presented a model for differentiated instruction in a mathematics class, based on revision of the traditional lesson plan that was presented in Box 3.1. However, others have recommended other approaches to differentiation such as the use of learning centers (Gregory, 2008). Clearly, differentiation can take many forms, but there are some common elements that seem to constitute our understanding of differentiated instruction today (Tomlinson, 2010). First, one might expect differentiated groups to be based more on similar learning capabilities and similar learning styles rather than exclusively on multiple intelligences theory. Further, technology is today playing a role in differentiation that could not have been imagined only ten years ago, and this trend is likely to continue for the foreseeable future. Finally, based on these factors, and the individualized instructional emphasis that is the basis for RTI, one might well expect either a significant decrease or the elimination of whole-group instruction, as teachers move increasingly toward highly interactive differentiated instructional activities.

> *Differentiation can take many forms, but there are some common elements that constitute differentiated instruction today.*

In this section, we present an example of a technology-rich reading class where individual attention is the norm and in which students receive intensive instruction in an RTI framework, as needed. Further, in this class, no whole-group instruction takes place. Rather, this model of differentiated instruction involves use of learning centers, and instruction is differentiated based on learning styles and formation of homogeneous reading groups. We should note that this is a fictitious example, but it is very similar to the manner in which the second author of this text taught her reading curriculum in a second-grade class (Bender & Waller, 2011).

What Learning Centers Should Be Set Up?

In establishing a technology-rich environment for differentiation in reading, a minimum of four learning centers should be established (of course, teachers are certainly free to set up more). In addition, the teacher worked with small, homogeneous groups of students at the teacher's worktable for most of the reading instructional period. For this example, we'll discuss four learning centers: the computer center, the spelling center, the writing center, and a poetry/literature center. In the computer center, six computers were located along one wall, and each held research-based software programs to teach both reading and mathematics.

In the spelling center, various activities were placed dealing with phonics, spelling patterns, and challenging spelling words. These included some worksheet activities as well as some activities intended for small groups or manipulative activities such as constructing a word from letters or syllables. When students left this center, they were instructed to place their work in their personal folders and take the folders with them to the next center. This allowed the teacher to review that "hardcopy" work after class.

In the writing center, students were challenged to write something every time they went to the center. Because this primary teacher taught the class around thematic units, the writing assignment often involved writing several sentences or, for more advanced students, a paragraph about the theme of the unit. When students left that center, they were to place their writing, either finished or unfinished, in their personal folder.

In the poetry and literature center, the teacher normally placed a poem, a story, or other literature that related to the thematic unit of the class. Students might be required to read the poem in pairs and discuss it together. Then they might individually write some type of reflection about that poem or story in their writing journals. In many cases, the assignments from the poetry/literature center and the writing center related to each other.

What Is in Each Learning Center?

Setting up the learning centers was relatively easy. Each included, at a minimum, a table by the wall to hold learning-center materials and a large poster label on the wall naming the center. The computer center, obviously, held the computers and appropriate software. Each center also held a small dry-erase board on which the teacher could write individual assignments for various students, or one assignment for the small group. Each center typically included a storage box, with ten to fifteen file folders in the box. Each file folder should have been labeled with the name and specific type of activity, and a number (e.g., Writing Center; Folder 12; Journal reflection on the poem, "The Tree"). Each folder would include a worksheet, manipulative activity, or directions for an activity, and each center activity was structured to require approximately fifteen minutes to complete.

How Should Differentiated Instructional Groups Be Established?

In a differentiated class, both heterogeneous and homogeneous groups may be formed for instruction, and both reading level and learning style strengths should be considered in formation of reading groups. However, because reading instruction typically takes place in homogeneous groups, this teacher divided her class into four homogeneous groups for reading.

This teacher used a PalmPilot-based reading assessment tool called mCLASS (www.wirelessgeneration.com/solutions/mclass-reading/html) as her universal screening assessment. This tool presents a running record of a student's reading, wherein the teacher follows along in a reading section that is presented on a PalmPilot, with the teacher noting all student errors directly on the PalmPilot as the student reads a story. This e-assessment tool then completes the scoring of the running record and downloads that record to the teacher's computer. The software identifies all types of errors, including substitution of words, mispronunciations, omitted words, and others, and then tabulates those errors and shows the teacher a scoring sheet for each individual student or for each student in the class.

> In a differentiated reading class, both heterogeneous and homogeneous groups may be formed for instruction, and both reading level and learning style strengths should be considered in formation of reading groups.

In this class, the teacher administered that running-record reading e-assessment to every student a minimum of three times each year and used that reading score, coupled with some attention to the learning style preferences of the students, to establish homogeneous groups for reading instruction. In particular, students with a bodily kinesthetic learning preference were frequently grouped together, even if their academic level was somewhat mismatched with others in that group.

How Did This Teacher Organize the Lessons?

To begin reading instruction each day, three of the four instructional groups went to a learning center and began the work assigned in that center. A paraprofessional in the class monitored students' academic work and behavior in the various learning centers. However, one of those three groups was always assigned to the computer center. The individualized reading assignments in that center served to provide high-quality guided reading instruction to each student at their individual level. Further, that software also served to keep those students focused on their learning task, so very little monitoring of the behavior for those students was necessary.

Of course, at the beginning of the year, these second-grade students were coached on how to read the learning-center assignment and begin the work process in each center. Still, within two months, these second graders got used to this procedure. Also, students were repeatedly encouraged to complete their assignments and check their work in each center during a fifteen- to twenty-minute time frame, because student groups changed centers every fifteen to twenty minutes. For worksheets and other hardcopy assignments, students placed their finished and checked work in their individual folders for the teacher to check at a later time.

Some teachers might wish to use a two-minute warning when preparing for the students to change learning centers. Two minutes prior to the end of the twenty-minute period allocated for one learning center, the teacher might say to the class, "Two-minute warning." This means that the class should draw their work to a close in that center and save that work either in their personal folder or on the computer software. After their work is saved and their books and materials are closed and restored in the center, students should be taught to face the teacher. When the teacher sees each child facing him or her, the teacher can assign the groups to the next learning center.

Intensive Instruction: The Teacher's Worktable

Using this system in her second-grade class, the second author of this text easily structured an opportunity for intensive, teacher-led small-group work with one of the homogeneous groups. When center work began, the teacher called one of the four homogeneous groups to her worktable and then worked with that group intensively for the next twenty-minute period. Thus, she was working with from four to six students at any given time. Of course, some groups composed of more challenged readers often needed more of the teacher's instructional time, so she planned to work with those groups daily. Other groups needed teacher-led, intensive instruction only three or four times a week, so that difference allowed the teacher more time with students who needed intensive assistance.

At the teacher's worktable, a supplemental reading curriculum designed for teacher-led small-group work was used. Using those curricula, this teacher worked with students specifically on their areas of reading weakness.

What Happens in the Computer Center?

In the computer center, students work individually on computers—reading stories and doing comprehension questions, or definition questions, and so on—while doing all of their work through the lessons presented in the software. In this example, the reading program delivered guided reading instruction based on short stories coupled with phonics activities, definitions activities, and literal and inferential comprehension questions associated with each story. In modern computerized reading curricula, each student is placed at his or her reading level based on an assessment built in to the curriculum itself. Thus, students were assigned to reading level stories at exactly their instructional level. Each day, they accessed their assignment by themselves in the computer center, after some degree of training at the beginning of the year. They then read a story on the computer and then completed the activities and comprehension questions associated with that story.

Because modern computer programs store information on exactly where every student is (i.e., which story they are reading, how they completed the phonics, or the results for the comprehension questions for that story), students could work independently and then save their work within the software. Thus, the teacher is free to evaluate students' work after class merely by opening the software program and reviewing student's work.

Modern software involves intensive diagnostic assessment and placement of the student in a series of reading stories. This author found that students, at least from Grade 2 up, can get on the computer, open their software for their story, and begin their work with little supervision. Also, computerized learning environments of this nature have a great track record of keeping most kids on task! Thus, in this center, every student was reading daily and doing phonics, comprehension, or other reading activities on their individual stories. Further, all modern reading software can produce a thorough progress monitoring page for each student or compare each student's progress with the progress of others in the class. In this example, the teacher printed out a student reading-skills diagnostic report each week for students that were struggling in reading and carefully monitored the progress of all of the other students.

But When Did This Teacher Teach Reading?

Using this learning-center approach to differentiated instruction, teachers never need to lead the whole group in reading instruction! In a differentiated lesson, students are no longer expected to read the same story along with the whole class. Further, in this type of differentiated instruction, the teacher becomes a planner and facilitator for everyone's reading instruction, and she worked with every student in some small-group format at least several times each week. However, in this example, the teacher never led a whole-group reading lesson. Of course, she could choose to do so if, for example, a specific lesson seemed to lend itself to whole-group work (e.g., a special group-project lesson on an upcoming holiday).

We believe that students taught in this differentiated fashion received a much higher quality instruction overall than they would in a whole-group reading lesson. In whole-group lessons, some students might drift off task, and the assignment might be somewhat mismatched with their exact educational needs. Even if a teacher divided the class into two reading groups, there is often a serious mismatch between reading content and the reading level for the more challenged readers in the class, so having four homogeneous groups doing differentiated assignments is much more responsive to student need than having the traditional "redbirds and bluebirds" reading groups.

Further, in this technology-rich classroom, the students' software-based guided reading lessons were exactly at their individual reading level, as was the supplemental, intensive instruction provided by the teacher. In both cases, such instruction was highly targeted and focused more explicitly on each student's exact reading needs. Again, we would suggest that this could represent a highly differentiated reading instruction model that meets the needs of today's diverse students in most general education classrooms.

When Was Reading Progress Assessed?

In this system, the teacher assessed progress in a variety of ways. As discussed previously, the mCLASS e-assessment was used as the universal screener, for comparison of each student to others in the class and for identifying the homogeneous groups. Also, the computerized guided reading–software assessed student progress daily, and the teacher could easily assess that assessment data. Next, in the intensive groups working at the teacher's worktable, the supplemental curricula typically have formative assessments built into the program, offering another indicator of individual student achievement. In this system, progress monitoring on a daily or weekly basis for the struggling readers was essentially built into the organization of the classroom, which is a significant advantage for this approach to differentiated instruction.

OTHER ADVANTAGES OF LEARNING-CENTER INSTRUCTION

There are a number of other advantages to using learning centers as the basis for differentiation. First, implementing differentiation through learning centers is an RTI-friendly reading instructional system. As mentioned already, every student was assessed almost continuously, and thus, for students in a Tier 2 or Tier 3 intensive intervention, progress monitoring added no extra assessment burden to the teacher. In fact, for actually delivering Tier 2 instruction, this teacher found that her learning-center system assisted her greatly.

In the formation of the homogeneous reading groups, the students that needed a Tier 2 intervention were very likely to be placed in a group by themselves. To deliver more intensive Tier 2 instruction for those students, this teacher arranged to teach that group for two consecutive twenty-minute instructional time periods each day rather than only one. In that fashion, they received much more intensive instruction directly within the teacher-led small-group work. To make that possible, the more advanced readers only worked with the teacher three times each week. However, those advanced readers didn't suffer greatly since they progressed nicely anyway, and the computer-based guided reading instruction kept providing significant reading challenges for them. Thus, they didn't need the intensive level of assistance from the teacher that the more challenged readers required. In that fashion, this differentiated instructional system made time for the general education teacher to provide highly intensive Tier 2 instruction for those that needed it, thus greatly facilitating RTI in this classroom.

Next, learning centers placed more of the responsibility for learning on the students (Gregory, 2008). As long as the teaching/learning process views students as passive learners (i.e., the targets of group lessons, lectures, or discussions lead for the whole class, by the teacher), only limited learning occurs among struggling students. However, a learning-center approach makes students responsible for their own learning activities. Further, with most students, having some choice among assignments in the learning centers is even more likely to foster active student participation and enhance learning overall.

Next, a learning-center approach is adaptable to many subject areas (Gregory, 2008). For example, in the class described previously with four learning centers, three of which were exclusively for reading, the teacher could easily add a learning center for mathematics calculations and a learning center for problem solving. The computer center, if equipped with appropriate software, can easily serve as a mathematics learning center as well as a reading learning center. In fact, in a primary or elementary classroom, the six learning centers that have been described here (i.e., computer center, spelling center, writing center, poetry/literature center, problem-solving center, and calculation center) allow a teacher the option of teaching virtually every subject in the curriculum. By using the writing center assignments to stress subjects such as science, history, and health activities, virtually every core curriculum area can be covered through these learning centers.

LEARNING CENTERS IN UPPER-GRADE SUBJECT AREA CLASSES

It would also be possible to deliver differentiation instruction through learning centers in higher-grade, departmentalized classes. As a certified history teacher for middle and high school, the first author of this book leans toward social studies examples, and we'll use such an example here. In short, we believe that using a combination of learning-center work, computer work, media presentations and production, and small-group project work, it is possible to teach a differentiated secondary subject without ever teaching a whole-group lesson. This example presents what such a differentiated social studies class in high school might look like.

First, in establishing learning centers for teachers in a departmentalized school, the teachers must consider all of the courses they teach in a given year when setting up learning centers. For example, a secondary social studies teacher might teach any of the following courses: U.S. history, civics, government, world history, geography, or economics. Thus, in a given year, a teacher might be teaching three sections of U.S. history, one section of world history, and two sections of geography. He or she might also teach some rather more esoteric elective courses related to social studies, such as culture in the Middle Ages, comparative revolutions, or archeology of the Native American tribes. Of course, learning centers in higher-grade classes cannot include content and activities that cover every topic as well as every other topic, but learning centers can be created in which the activities cover most of the necessary curricular areas. Therefore, a secondary teacher, given his or her expertise in those broad social studies areas, should select learning-center titles that cut across those areas.

Learning centers with broad topics that represent themes that run throughout history and across cultures would seem to provide one option. For example, a learning center titled "Setting Impacting People" would be a good topical learning center for both history and geography classes. One theme in the general social studies area is that all peoples are products of their setting. Japan, as one example, developed a robust fishing tradition throughout their history, as it is a small island. England developed a large navy between 1700 and 1940 for the same reason: its island location, and the need for national defense in that country dictated such a navy. In contrast, neither Austria nor Germany ever developed a strong navy and maintained one over time, because those were basically landlocked nations. Rather, those nations developed strong military traditions based on large, land-based armies. Thus, a learning center on "Setting Impacting People" could cover topics in virtually every unit in world history, U.S. history, various state history courses, geography, and perhaps economics. This would be the type of learning center that could easily be used by a secondary social studies teacher in many subjects.

Another learning center that might cover a number of topics in these courses might be "Science, Mathematics, and Technology." While these may seem like strange topics for a social studies learning center, the fact is these are indicators of overall sociological development. When studying cultures or tribal groups of people, understanding of their scientific achievements, their level of technology, and their development of mathematics can tell much about their overall level of development as a society. Topics covered in that learning center can range across the board of scientific achievements: Did a given society develop use of the wheel? Did they develop mathematics? Did they develop high levels of architecture (e.g., the pyramid builders had highly developed mathematics that would allow for such construction)?

Like the elementary class described previously, a secondary social studies class should have a computer learning center, and that center should be in constant use. Assignments could emphasize webquests as individual or small-group projects, or production of multimedia presentations about various topics under study.

To make this learning-center idea work in a ninth- through twelfth-grade social studies class, the same organizational ideas and procedures should be used. The class should be divided into three to five homogeneous groups for their learning-center work, and one group would always be assigned to work in the computer center. Another group might be assigned to work with the teacher on intensive instruction using the text or other appropriate resources. The other students in the class could be involved in various individual or small-group projects in the other centers. However, unlike the elementary class described previously, most middle and secondary general education classes do not include a paraprofessional, so the teacher would have to monitor and facilitate the work of the students in the learning centers that were not working on computers, and this might preclude the option of teachers working with all groups every day.

Still, the main point here is that differentiation through learning centers will work in the higher grades in most, if not all, core classes. Thus, this approach to differentiation offers the option of decreasing significantly or eliminating whole-group instruction in favor of highly differentiated lessons. Again, the combination of judicious use of instructional technology, coupled with highly differentiated lesson activities that actively engage students in the learning process, is the key. On that basis, there is no rationale for holding whole-group lessons, even in the higher grades, unless the subject content requires whole-group lessons for a particular topic (e.g., classwide discussions of critical social studies events in the national news).

CONCLUSIONS

As educators, we realize that we tread on sacred ground in writing this text, and in particular in writing this chapter. We clearly advocate for the end of whole-group instruction, in contrast to Dr. Tomlinson, the originator of the differentiated instruction concept, who has not advocated that. However, with the changes stemming from the recent RTI initiative, increasing implementation of technology-based instruction, and the ongoing move to highly differentiated instruction throughout general education, we see the near-elimination of whole-group lessons as the inevitable evolution of education. A few pertinent questions help to illustrate that.

In considering the future of education, does anyone not believe that by 2050, all students will undertake all of their education endeavors with a laptop placed on their desk immediately before them? Will they not be doing assignments, either individually or in small groups, that tax their academic skills to the maximum, rather than listening to lectures or passively viewing videos? Will they not be creating content via individual and group projects, that allow them to experience the content in a new, and wholly different, fashion? Finally, if these examples represent the future of education, why not now?

Further, in a 21st-century world, shouldn't highly differentiated, or even totally individualized, lessons be the basis for our instruction? Should we retain an age-based instructional system, in which persons are placed in classes and whole-group lessons when their only similarity is that they happen to be the same general chronological age? Is this really our best approach to modern education?

Finally, why would anyone want to perpetuate an instructional system that does not teach students even the basics of technology applications for today, not to mention technology applications that seem to be evolving for tomorrow? What should be our ultimate aim, the primary goal for our educational endeavors, if not to prepare students for their future?

Again, we believe that the massive wave of change brought about by the interactions of the RTI initiative, modern technology applications, and the differentiated instructional movement is already upon us. Classrooms must begin to look and feel quite different in this brave new world, and increased differentiation of instructional activities is the foundation of this upheaval. As Tomlinson and her coauthors indicated, differentiation is a second-order change, requiring a reshaping of one's belief systems about what teaching is. Wilmarth (2010) indicated that technology was going to redefine our teaching/learning process, and taken together, these changes will be profound. Clearly, the concept of highly differentiated instruction is the basis for it all. Thus, not only is differentiated instruction the necessary basis for effective Tier 1 instruction; it also represents the next evolution in the teaching/learning process.

Of course, these changes find their ultimate expression in a totally independent, technology-driven curriculum where students choose their assignments and study what interests them. This again reflects several of the imaginings delineated in the Introduction, but it also begins to approach what the teaching/learning process might look like in 2015, or 2050, or 2100. We advocate that educators embrace this change, for to aim any lower than this is to do a disservice not only to our students' futures but also to ourselves as professional educators.

The next question, however, is, where does this lofty goal of embracing these changes leave educators today? What might educators today do to prepare for these changes? How should educators shift their instructional practices, given these changes in the teaching/learning process?

Of course, predicting the specifics of a massive reform effort, particularly one involving multiple change agents, is rarely a winnable scenario. Still, as authors, we believe we must attempt to share some thoughts on where these changes may take us all over the next decade. The next chapter presents a set of recently developed instructional practices that are much more commensurate with highly differentiated instruction and are rooted in technology more so than the traditional lesson plan. Further, these innovations in instruction are tied more concretely to real-world learning. Thus, in the next chapter, we seek to put these changes—RTI, technology, and differentiated instruction—into the context of today's and tomorrow's classroom practices.

4 The Dynamic Synthesis

Instructional Strategies for the
21st-Century Classroom

A SYNTHESIS OF COMMON DIRECTIONS

Given the restructuring of learning and instructional practices that is likely to occur as a result of the dynamic synthesis of RTI, technology, and differentiated instruction, we wanted to present some discussion of what this synthesis might mean for classroom practices. Also, based on that dynamic synthesis, we discuss in this chapter several modern instructional strategies that might fit within the broader texture of the 21st-century classroom. While prediction of change is always problematic, a synthesis of the current trends in RTI, technology, and differentiated instruction can suggest various types of instructional activities that might meet the needs of students in the 21st century better than today's instructional practices. Here are several similarities between and among these three change factors that seem to be leading toward similar instructional practices. These are the factors that enhance the cumulative impact of the three sisters.

> *While prediction of change is always problematic, current trends in RTI, technology, and differentiated instruction can suggest various types of instructional activities that might meet the needs of students in the 21st century better than today's instructional practices.*

First, the explosive growth of technology in the area of social networking, the dramatic increase in the numbers of students using those technologies, and the energy and excitement that those students show for that type of collaborative endeavor suggest that learning paradigms of the future will be much more social in nature (Ferriter & Garry, 2010; Wilmarth, 2010). Current estimates suggest that today's adolescent spends an average of fifty hours each week engaged with digital media in one form or another (Dretzin, 2011), and the impact of such extensive engagement has lead proponents to advocate "reaching students where they live" by drastically increasing these to questions concerning addiction to the Internet. The social nature of these media (MySpace, Twitter, Facebook, computer gamming, etc.) is a critically important part of their popularity (Dretzin, 2011). In fact, Silver and Perini (2010) have suggested that social learning may be one of the fundamental styles of learning among students today. Clearly, learning activities that have some basis in collaborative or social-networking learning opportunities based in part on these modern technologies should be considered as instructional approaches of the future (Ferriter & Garry, 2010), while careful attention must also be given to potential problems that may emerge from such instruction (Dretzin, 2011).

Not only technology but also differentiated instruction tends to increase the social nature of learning processes. Differentiated instruction has often been described as based, in part, on grouping of students such that learning can take place in a social context (Bender, 2008; Chapman & King, 2005; Tomlinson, 2010; Tomlinson, Brimijoin, & Narvaez, 2008). In that sense, both today's digital communications technologies and the move toward increased differentiation of instruction are pushing us toward more socially based learning.

However, the move toward learning in the social context should not merely be interpreted as increased small-group work. Rather, as technologies are applied in the classroom, the very nature of the teaching/learning process changes, with the teacher functioning more like a facilitator of learning and students taking increased responsibility for collaborative constructions of knowledge (Drake & Long, 2009; Ferriter & Garry, 2010; Wilmarth, 2010). While traditional learning was rather passive in nature (i.e., the textbook, the teacher, or the Internet provided information to students), today's technology applications foster and facilitate much more active learning in which students collaboratively explore a problem and then create content for immediate and worldwide publication (Ferriter & Garry, 2010). This tends to make students much more active in the learning process than merely playing the role of passive recipients of knowledge, and again, this changes the teaching/learning process.

> *Students using the newly emerging instructional technologies are actually producing content for publication on the web or for presentation in the classroom, and this tends to make students much more active in the learning process than merely playing the role of passive recipients of knowledge.*

Next, one might well anticipate that some changes in assessment practices will emerge from the synthesis of RTI, differentiated instruction, and technology. Specifically, each of these areas seem increasingly directed toward increased, highly specific, individual assessments of a formative nature rather than summative assessments for the whole class (i.e., unit tests) or large-scale local or statewide assessment programs (Bender, 2009; Chapman & King, 2005; Marzano, 2010a). For example, RTI stresses highly individualistic universal screening to help make instructional decisions. For students in higher tiers of the RTI process, individual progress monitoring assessments are administered weekly or every two weeks, as a general rule (Bender, 2009a).

> *One might well anticipate that the synthesis of RTI, differentiated instruction, and technology will increasingly emphasize highly specific, individual assessments of a formative nature rather than summative assessments for the whole class or large-scale local or statewide assessment programs.*

This emphasis on individualized formative assessments for instructional purposes is likewise stressed in modern computer-based instructional curricula. In fact, nearly every computer-based instructional package discussed in this text involves an individually administered screening and diagnostic assessment that is used to place students into the specific lessons that the student needs. Even the differentiated instructional approach emphasizes more focused, formative assessment practices (Chapman & King, 2005). Of course, differentiated instruction has always advocated highly differentiated instructional activities for various students with different learning styles, but more recently, that discussion of differentiated instruction has led to an emphasis on differentiated assessments within a given class (Bender, 2008; Chapman & King, 2005; Tomlinson, 2010; Tomlinson et al., 2008). In short, each of these factors—RTI, technology, and differentiation—seems to support the increasing emphasis identified by Marzano (2010a, 2010b) as the shift toward increased use of formative assessment.

With these examples of what this synthesis of RTI, technology, and differentiation might mean, we can now consider instructional approaches that might be more appropriate for the classrooms of the future than traditional instructional paradigms. This chapter presents three instructional approaches we recommend for the modern classroom. While a wide variety of computerized curricula are available today (indeed, we have described several of those elsewhere in this book), in this chapter, we have chosen to present instructional procedures that are not exclusively or even primarily based on computerized instruction. We made this choice to show that not all 21st-century instruction will involve totally independent applications of computerized instructional programs, and indeed, much of the instruction in the next century will be social and collaborative in nature.

While none of these instructional strategies are new—indeed, these instructional strategies have been around for one or two decades—they are the types of instruction that fit within the changes described in previous chapters and that are likely to be brought about over the next decade (Partnership for 21st Century Skills, 2009a; Wilmarth, 2010). These instructional strategies include project-based learning, cooperative learning, and peer tutoring. In each case, the strategy is presented along with specific guidelines on implementation in various subjects and/or at different grade levels. Also, each strategy is discussed in light of the types of 21st-century skills that can be developed using these instructional approaches.

Of course, other strategies may well address the needs and design of the changing classroom also, and we do not suggest that these three are the only instructional tactics that will be used in schools of the future. However, we are confident that the use of these strategies is likely to increase rather dramatically, in that the three factors precipitating the coming changes in the teaching/learning process strongly suggest such an increase. In some cases, advocates for these changes specifically recommend increased use of these three strategies. For example, the Partnership for 21st Century Skills (2009a) advocacy group not only recommends increased integration of technology in every classroom but also strongly supports project-based learning as an instructional paradigm that is consistent with future demands of the classroom and the world at large. Also, both that Partnership and various proponents of differentiated instruction recommend increased use of peer tutoring and cooperative instructional approaches (Bender, 2008; Partnership for 21st Century Skills, 2009b; Tomlinson, 2010).

PROJECT-BASED LEARNING: INSTRUCTION FOR THE FUTURE

What Is Project-Based Learning?

Project-based learning (PBL) is an innovative instructional method that centers on the learners confronting a critical problem or project for which no single solution exists (Cole & Wasburn-Moses, 2010; Fleischner & Manheimer, 1997; Grant, 2002; Knowlton, 2003; Marzano, 2007). The process of solving the problem or completing the project should move students collectively toward development of personally meaningful projects or artifacts that address the guiding questions that provide the basis for the assignment (Grant, 2002; Rhem, 1998). Over the years, various names have been used for this type of instructional technique, including problem-based learning, inquiry learning, authentic learning, and discovery learning. Still, the overall concept remains the same: students seeking to solve real-world problems that they consider important and developing various artifacts to present and communicate their problem solution (Bender & Crane, 2010; Cole & Wasburn-Moses, 2010; Fleischner & Manheimer, 1997; Knowlton, 2003; Marzano, 2007).

> *PBL centers on the learners confronting a critical problem or project for which no single solution exists and moving toward the problem's solution collectively.*

PBL engages the students through focusing on one or more highly motivating questions or problems that students perceive as worthwhile. In many projects, the problem itself may be framed as a guiding question or a central-problem-based task that does not have a simple solution (Grant, 2002). In some PBL projects, there might be several solutions that can be reached, depending on the varying strategies selected by the group completing the project (Ghosh, 2010). Once a guiding question, problem, or project is determined, students working together will then engage in a complex series of tasks to move toward a solution to the problem. These tasks typically include

- brainstorming solutions to the problem;
- designing a series of tasks to move the group toward a possible solution;
- searching for information on the problem or question;
- synthesizing that information;
- problem solving and collaborative decision making on how to move forward; and
- developing a product, or multiple products or artifacts, that allows students to communicate the results of their work.

While projects vary considerably, nearly all are focused on an actual problem or issue from the real world, and often students have some say in selecting those projects or delineating the problem under study. They then develop a plan of action and begin to develop their products or artifacts. In many cases, development of those products or artifacts will involve actual creation of a presentation, video demonstration, a working model, or a test-model for their project or problem (Bender & Crane, 2010; Grant, 2002; Land & Green, 2000; Partnership for 21st Century Skills, 2004, 2009b). A project may be targeted toward one subject area or it might be interdisciplinary in nature (Grant, 2002; Land & Green, 2000). Because students typically have some involvement in how the problem is stated, or how the project is planned, they often become progressively more motivated and ultimately take on additional responsibilities for their own education (http://www.pbli.org/pbl/pbl.htm).

In that sense, PBL serves as an answer for critics who claim students are not prepared for corporate life after college as this instructional strategy uses real-world, complex problems to teach standards and content in the classroom. In this instructional approach, students are given or develop a challenging, relatively complex problem for their project that resembles tasks adults might face in the real world (Fleischner & Manheimer, 1997; Knowlton, 2003). Students are required to work together in small groups to address the issue and to implement feasible solutions. Essentially, this is the process of collaborative work in industry and business, and students take on the role of a scientist, working to find solutions to the problem that they are investigating (Drake & Long, 2009).

> *In PBL students are given or develop a challenging, relatively complex problem for their project that resembles tasks adults might face in the real world.*

Of course, various proponents of PBL emphasize different advantages of this instructional approach (Drake & Long, 2009; Fleischner & Manheimer, 1997; Grant, 2002). However, the social nature of this instruction approach is apparent in virtually all descriptions of PBL. For example, the Project on the Effectiveness of Project Based Learning identified three criteria that summarize these aspects of PBL: curriculum that is built around problems with an emphasis on cognitive skills and knowledge, a student-centered learning environment that uses small groups and active learning where teachers serve as facilitators, and student outcomes focused on the development of skills, motivation, and a love for lifelong learning (Drake & Long, 2009).

The model of PBL teaches students how to learn by encouraging them to participate in research, investigation, and the application of new knowledge (Rule & Barrera, 2008). Essentially, PBL forces students to create meaning in the form of a solution to the problem, or project, using the data they collect as opposed to simply collecting facts as passive listeners (Rhem, 1998). Further, the integration of various subject areas with various thinking skills in PBL helps teachers work through overloaded content requirements by teaching students to see the connectedness of various curriculum areas (Rule & Barrera, 2008). Likewise, PBL projects today involve heavy use of various technologies for research (e.g., Internet searches, webquests), or creation of artifacts (e.g., blog posting, wikis, or presentations developed via computer).

What Does a PBL Assignment Look Like?

Box 4.1 presents a sample PBL for study of water usage in a middle school context. One can see the interdisciplinary nature of this project, as various areas of study are involved including ecology, science, conservation, and politics. Further, by adding requirements to this project (e.g., calculations of future growth of the number of households in the city over the next ten years), one can make this project more complex and involve additional subject areas.

In planning a PBL project, teachers should consider developing a rubric to let students know what is expected and to help students set parameters that focus their activities. Giving students a rubric gives them a starting point as to the teacher's expectations and the overall needs of the project.

Box 4.1   **Setting Water Usage Guidelines in Your Town, USA**

A PBL Sample

The state is in a drought condition; rainfall has not been adequate to keep up with demand. The mayor of your city has been told by the state government that his city will receive only 2 million gallons of water daily for household use, but local industry must receive 1.7 million or workers will be laid off. Therefore, only the remaining water is available for households each day, and there are 14,873 households in the town. The mayor has asked that everyone conserve as much water as possible, and the mayor wants to provide guidelines for each family. Of course, many community members are grumbling about the request while they wash their cars, water their lawns, and play on Slip 'n Slides. The mayor has reminded persons of the typical requirements of water, by presenting the following charted information. However, if community members are not invested in the cause, water conservation will not happen in your city. The mayor needs to see your recommendation for average current and recommended household water usage. Remember that these guidelines may become mandatory in the near future.

Typical Water Usage in A Typical Household

Flushing a commode—takes 3 gallons of water
Washing dishes in a dishwasher—takes 3 gallons of water
Washing a single load of clothes—takes 4 gallons of water
One ten minute shower—takes 3 gallons of water
Watering an average lawn—takes 7 gallons of water
Washing a car—takes 3 gallons of water
Other Activities (watering plants, cooking)—takes 8 gallons of water

Tasks to Be Accomplished: Students will work in groups together to accomplish several tasks:

(Continued)

(Box 4.1 Continued)

1. Using students in the class as examples, generate data about current water usage. Students should determine how much water each student's household may use on a daily basis. They will be required to gather that information and turn it in as a spreadsheet.

2. Determine the relationship between the number of persons living in a household and the water usage of that household, using the data collected from the students' homes as examples.

3. Develop an average of water usage based on their numbers, and then develop an average water usage number based on population of city.

4. Determine how much water a single household will receive under the water limitations in the problem.

5. Develop a plan to limit water usage in the city.

6. Create a multimedia presentation that will persuade community members to join in the cause and limit/conserve water.

Students will need access to

1. computers with Microsoft Office, PowerPoint, videos, and cameras;

2. databases with current populations listed, household composition, etc.

However, PBL projects are not necessarily as long term as the project presented in Box 4.1. Indeed, some projects may take only a few periods or portions of instructional periods to complete. Imagine, for example, a teacher in a fourth-grade classroom involved in a study of the solar system. She might create cooperative learning groups in which each group was responsible for a presentation discussing planets and other bodies in the solar system. In this example, the teacher might create a heterogeneous group that includes a strong reader, a strong writer, a technology-savvy student, a weaker reader who nevertheless has some skill in using the Internet, and a well-organized student leader. In that example, each member in the group would be able to use his or her own personal strengths to achieve the group goal while also learning from the rest of the group.

How Do I Implement PBL?

In a classroom where PBL is implemented, the teacher plays the role of a facilitator and works to guide students in the process of analyzing, researching, and ultimately solving the problem (Grant, 2002), and this represents a change from the traditional teaching role of information-delivery agent as in a lecture-based instructional approach. In essence, the teacher becomes a coach that oversees and ultimately facilitates the problem-solving process (Rule & Barrera, 2008). Facilitating instruction in this context may include orchestrating selection of meaningful problems, providing adequate resources, coaching students on use of specific research tools (e.g., the Internet, YouTube, etc.), suggesting additional effective research strategies, and being available to provide assistance as students work through the process. Of course, teachers have always undertaken this facilitative role to some degree in various projects within the traditional class, but in PBL, this role becomes the primary instructional role rather than an occasional emphasis.

> *In PBL, the teacher plays the role of a facilitator and works to guide students in the process of analyzing, researching, and ultimately solving the problem.*

Given this role change, preparation for using PBL as a basis for instruction involves more than merely selecting a problem and planning a project. To prepare for PBL, teachers should initially consider their comfort level for this somewhat less structured instructional format. Because student insights and understandings will need time to evolve, teachers should recognize that rushing students toward a particular answer is not advisable in the PBL approach, and some teachers may sense a loss of control of the classroom for that reason. To move comfortably into PBL, we recommend that teachers begin PBL by selecting the class or subject area in which they are most comfortable. If an elementary teacher has a strength for and love of mathematics, perhaps the initial PBL should be undertaken in that subject area. In that way, teachers can then learn the PBL teaching approach in an area in which they are comfortable and then move toward increased PBL instruction in other areas later.

Next, we recommend that teachers move into PBL by undertaking more limited instructional projects initially. Rather that dive into a long-term project such as that presented in Box 4.1, teachers may wish to initiate a shorter project that takes only five to six sessions of thirty minutes each to complete. In that fashion, the teacher will gain some experience in facilitating a PBL learning environment but will not lose much instructional time if the initial project goes awry.

Next, teachers should talk to others in their school or district about PBL and identify other teachers that are doing projects in their classes.

Box 4.2   **Websites for PBL**

http://pbl-online.org—This is a site related to the Buck Institute that provides information on how to design PBL projects using five sequenced tasks: begin with the end in mind, craft the driving question, plan the assessment, map the project, and manage the process.

www.bie.org—This is the website for the Buck Institute for Education, which is a nonprofit corporation dedicated to PBL. This site can offer materials for purchase in PBL as well as professional development opportunities for PBL.

www.Edutopia.org/project-based-learning—This site offers several short videos, including a three-minute video titled "Introduction to Project Based Learning," and a nine-minute video, "Project Based Learning: An Overview." One can also join the new online magazine focusing on PBL "and design."

http://imet.csus.edu/imet2/stanfillj/workshops/pbl/description .htm—This site is perhaps the single richest resource on PBL in that many other sites are linked. One can find many examples of PBL projects, and information on how projects may be designed and implemented.

http://www.internet4classrooms.com/project.htm—This site provides a compendium of other links that can support PBL. Examples include a site of biographies of famous persons in a variety of areas (science, history, politics), as well as sites providing statistics on various countries. This site should be provided as a resource directly to students in many middle and high school PBL projects.

Perhaps teachers can arrange to observe various examples of PBL in their school. Likewise, teachers should search the Internet for PBL projects at their grade level and in the subject they have selected. By reading through projects completed in other classrooms, teachers can get a sense of what PBL will involve in terms of not only how much time a particular project might require but also the level of supports that might be necessary for students undertaking that or a similar project. In addition to the sample project presented already, Box 4.2 presents a list of websites that provide information or sample PBL projects that teachers might review.

Another concern for teachers moving into PBL involves how to fit long-term PBL projects into their class. While the more traditional unit-based instruction often focuses on only one small set of information (e.g., an instructional unit on the American Revolution), a PBL project might involve a much broader topic and much more information overall (e.g.,

what causes civilian populations to stage a revolution against their government?). Thus, one question becomes, "When should I undertake that
project?" Further, most projects do require an array of content knowledge
that is typically longer than a given instructional unit.

In addressing a project on what causes civilian populations to stage
a revolution against the government, students might need to know how
to collect data on various revolutions or calculate average food consump-
tion or tax rates, if those are deemed to be causal factors. Students might
then need to create spreadsheets to summarize a portion of their research
or write a one-act play to demonstrate why revolutions might take place.
Teachers will need to be creative in fitting this type of project into the U.S.
or world history class, and that project might take place over several different units of study. Teachers must look at the problem and their required
curriculum to determine an appropriate "fit" for each PBL activity. Also,
the PBL activity can be modified somewhat to fit within parameters determined by the teacher and students.

In moving into PBL, teachers have two options: part-time PBL or full-
time PBL. First, many teachers implement PBL on the basis of splitting their
instructional period. In the first half of the instructional period, traditional
unit-based instruction might be undertaken, whereas work on the PBL
project might fill the remaining time each period. Alternatively, teachers
organize their days so that certain days are designated for traditional unit-
based teaching and others are reserved for the PBL assignment. Second,
some teachers have undertaken PBL as the basis for all of their instruction
(Grant, 2002). In such an instructional approach, PBL actually replaces the
more traditional unit-based instructional practices, such as the common
practice of covering the Civil War in a two-week instructional unit, or covering invertebrates in a two-week unit prior to moving on to a two-week
unit on vertebrates. In this approach, teachers actually replace unit-based
instruction with PBL for a semester or the entire year. Of course, teachers using this PBL approach will need to carefully consider the learning
standards to be covered and make certain that each individual standard
is addressed in some fashion within some project during a given year. In
this way, not only will differentiated instruction free teachers and students
from whole-group instruction; coupled with PBL, it will free teachers and
students from unit-based instruction as well. Given the traditional depen-
dence on whole-group lesson planning and unit-based instruction, these
changes are nothing less than revolutionary.

> *In moving into PBL, teachers have two options: part-time PBL or full-
> time PBL.*

Of course, teachers always have to make certain that the activities in
a PBL series of lessons are worthwhile learning activities and that the students don't merely get "stuck" traveling the information superhighway.

Thus, questions and problems need to be highly focused, specific task directions will need to be either provided by the teacher or identified by the students as part of the problem-solution process, and rubrics should typically be provided to give more guidance to students. In fact, some teachers in PBL classes use rubrics to differentiate among the groups, with very complete, specific rubrics provided for some students, while highly advanced students might undertake the project with less guidance and/or no rubric at all. A sample rubric for the water usage problem is presented in Box 4.3.

Box 4.3   Rubric for Water Usage Guidelines Project

Stated Objective	1	2	3	4
Team must compile individual data on household water usage and complete a spreadsheet for the team.	Team gathered and compiled individual data but did not complete a suitable spreadsheet.	Team gathered and compiled individual data. Team compiled data in a spreadsheet with minimal organization.	Team gathered and compiled individual data. Team created a spreadsheet that was easy to read and organized.	Team gathered and compiled individual data. Team created a spreadsheet that was organized, well labeled, color coded, and easy to interpret.
Team must develop an average water usage for their team and then calculate average water usage for community.	Team did not use appropriate formulas for collecting and analyzing data.	Team used appropriate formulas but came up with incorrect answers.	Team used appropriate formulas and came up with accurate data.	Team used appropriate formulas, provided accurate data, and compared data across various subgroups in community.
Team must develop a plan to limit water usage.	Team's plan was not sufficiently detailed. Water usage would only slightly be limited.	Team's plan was adequate but was not organized in a feasible way.	Team had an appropriately detailed plan that would adequately limit water usage in a feasible way.	Team's plan was detailed with several strategies for limiting water usage.
Team must present a multimedia presentation that will persuade community members to participate.	Presentation only integrated one type of technology and was not convincing.	Presentation integrated two technologies and was persuasive but not personal enough to incite action.	Presentation integrated three technologies and was personal for each community member.	Presentation integrated four technologies. The details were persuasive and personal. Community members would have signed up!

Developing Higher-Order Cognitive Skills in PBL

Teachers undertaking PBL often want assurances that this instructional approach can stress deeper conceptual understanding (Rule & Barrera, 2008). One way to address this concern in the context of PBL involves providing scaffolded instructional support on specific thinking skills for students as they work through an ill-defined problem (Rule & Barrera, 2008). Some authors recommend use of the Cognitive Research Trust (CoRT) Thinking Skills lessons (de Bono, 2009) in conjunction with PBL (Rule & Barrera, 2008). CoRT Thinking Skills were introduced in 1970 by Edward de Bono and consist of lessons that ultimately help students improve their thinking (de Bono, 2009; see also www.edwdebono.com/cort). The thinking lessons may be implemented based on either a teacher or a school license (www.cortthinking.com), and the entire system is composed of some sixty sequenced lessons in six different areas. Each lesson teaches a new set of thinking skills. The six broad areas, referred to as CoRT 1 through CoRT 6, include breadth, organization, interaction, creativity, information and feeling, and actions.

The first set of lessons focus on breadth of thinking and include specific lesson activities on determining plusses and minuses; considering all factors, consequences, and sequels; other people's views; first important priorities; alternatives, possibilities, and choices; aims, goals, and objectives; and planning, decisions, and rules (Rule & Barrera, 2008). Once students have mastered these basis thinking skills, the teacher can determine which additional skills should be stressed for individual students, and the lessons can be differentiated on that basis.

For instance, some students might need to focus on CoRT 2, lessons on organization, while others may need to focus on CoRT 5, information and feeling. The CoRT lessons allow a teacher to teach the thinking skills in the context of a project or problem that would enable students to practice the newly acquired skills. Learning a new set of thinking skills prior to introducing a new PBL problem ensures that the students are prepared to work through the problem scenario and gives the teacher a sense of confidence as students implement newly acquired thinking skills.

What Are the Advantages of PBL?

As seen in the preceding example, problems used for PBL activities involve real-world scenarios, and this typically increases the students' interest in the work that is required (Grant, 2002; Partnership for 21st Century Skills, 2009a, 2009c). In this particular problem, the integration of content from subject areas, technology, and a concrete problem results in a stronger understanding of the content overall. PBL results in deeper, richer instruction, which in turn leads to stronger connections between the varying content areas. The sample problem integrates understanding from multiple content areas. Students are required to work in small groups, which strengthens oral communication skills; to use mathematical understanding to generate averages; to research and compile data and statistics; to use oral and written skills to persuade community members; and to use technology to create a multimedia presentation. As the sample shows, the experience the students go through is truly similar to problems adults face on a daily basis. The meaningful and relevant problem will typically result in higher student interest and motivation.

> *Problems used in PBL activities involve real-world scenarios, and this typically increases the students' interest in the work that is required.*

There are other advantages that result from the implementation of PBL in the classroom. PBL is a differentiated instructional approach (Bender & Crane, 2010) that allows teachers to challenge and remediate where needed. PBL tasks can be tailored to fit student need and interest, with some students focusing on direct data collection and research, while others develop artifacts such as role-play activities, multimedia presentations, or creative tasks. For example, using the sample PBL project provided, those students needing enrichment might be required to create and edit a podcast as part of their multimedia presentation. That would force students to create a script that incorporated persuasive writing techniques to develop the arguments on water conservation. Students needing intervention and remediation in various reading or research skills might be required to create a blog as part of their responsibilities. The shorter format for blog writing might provide a chance for struggling students to incorporate persuasive writing without the intimidation of longer essays.

PBL also provides the opportunity for richer content coverage as curriculum is integrated into meaningful problems. In the example in this chapter, students are researching, synthesizing information, and creating presentations using technology. Students are able to see the interconnectedness of the learning that they are doing and the relevance of that work to real-world problems.

PBL creates higher rates of active engagement with content (Grant, 2002). As a result, students show more excitement about learning—wanting to know more and do more based on PBL assignments (Partnership for 21st Century Skills, 2007). The real-world learning experiences designed to simulate work-like situations develop problem-solving skills for students. This ultimately results in an increase in achievement (Fleischner & Manheimer, 1997; Grant, 2002; Knowlton, 2003; Partnership for 21st Century Skills, 2007). One research summary indicated that students might improve as much as 30 percent in their understanding of concepts as a result of PBL (Gijbels, Dochy, Van den Bossche, & Segers, 2005). Another study conducted in two fourth-grade classrooms found that students participating in the PBL activity had 4.27 more minutes of on-task, engaged science instruction (as compared to the control group) per 45 minutes of class instruction, resulting in 12.8 hours of active science instruction over the course of the year (Drake & Long, 2009).

Although PBL requires labor-intensive planning, the results given indicate it is well worth it for the students (Bender & Crane, 2010; Fleischner & Manheimer, 1997). The positive data and research have resulted in an increasing number of schools incorporating PBL assignments into their curriculum (Fleischner & Manheimer, 1997; Grant, 2002; Partnership for 21st Century Skills, 2007; Strobel & van Barneveld, 2009), and some of these have actually replaced instructional units with a series of instructional projects for a given year. It is vital that general education teachers begin looking at possible ways to implement PBL in their classrooms as part of their Tier 1 instruction.

Why Is PBL Recommended for 21st-Century Classes?

The Partnership for 21st Century Skills strongly supports PBL for a variety of reasons. While the various examples provided of PBL are quite diverse, the research, as already noted, indicates that this tactic is effective in keeping students involved with their learning. Further, modern instructional technologies make collaborative work on learning projects possible in ways that would not have been possible only a decade ago. Next, because PBL is multifaceted and typically involves a wide variety of necessary tasks, teachers can differentiate instruction in this paradigm quite easily, and several examples were provided in the preceding discussion.

Finally, because of the communication and collaboration necessary in this instructional format, various proponents of PBL suggest that this teaching method more closely approximates real-world working environments of the next century (Fleischner & Manheimer, 1997; Grant, 2002; Partnership for 21st Century Skills, 2009a). Thus, skills such as workplace collaboration, teaming, and committee work are strengthened in this approach more so than in more traditional instructional models.

COOPERATIVE LEARNING

What Is Cooperative Learning?

Cooperative learning involves having students learn in a collaborative, cooperative fashion, rather than independently (Adams & Hamm, 1994; Johnson, Johnson, & Smith, 1991, 2007; Tsay & Brady, 2010). Teachers have long recognized that students will often pay more attention to other students than they will to teachers, so delivery of instructional content can be accomplished by having students share information with each other. Like the PBL instructional approach described previously, cooperative learning is precipitated on students working together to build each other's understanding (Adams & Hamm, 1994; Tsay & Brady, 2010).

Of course, cooperative learning approaches may well be a part of a PBL instructional approach, but cooperative learning procedures may also stand alone as one collaborative instructional approach that virtually every teacher in any subject area can implement. Also, while PBL projects, as discussed already, typically involve implementation over long periods of time, many cooperative learning tactics can be completed in a single instructional period.

> *Cooperative learning is precipitated on students working together to build each other's understanding.*

The words *cooperative* and *learning* can scare many teachers. Just the phrase *cooperative groups* conjures up pictures of messy classrooms, noisy students, arguments, and off-task behavior. However, when implemented and used correctly, cooperative learning can be a beneficial, and relatively structured, instructional strategy. In a classroom where cooperative learning is taking place, one can observe small groups of students working together to help each other learn the academic content (Johnson et al., 2007; Tsay & Brady, 2010). Successful cooperative learning is certainly more organized and must incorporate several elements, including positive interdependence, face-to-face interaction, accountability, interpersonal skills, and group processing. Further, cooperative learning is built on the idea that students learn through social contexts and through interaction with their environment (Adams & Hamm, 1994; Johnson et al., 2007; Tsay & Brady, 2010). Thus, cooperative learning provides an opportunity for students to interact with their peers to make sense of the new material they are given (Johnson et al., 2007; Tsay & Brady, 2010).

Cooperative learning groups must be interdependent (Johnson et al., 2007; Tsay & Brady, 2010); students in small cooperative learning groups should be working together to achieve a common goal and must rely on one another to achieve that goal. Also, differentiated instruction is facilitated when teachers implement cooperative learning approaches. In fact, when creating cooperative learning groups, teachers can ensure that students with various strengths and weaknesses are placed together to facilitate successful group interactions. By doing this, each student will sense that they have a unique contribution to make because of their own personal resources and talents.

For cooperative learning groups to be successful, time must be provided for students to work together, allowing for questions, challenges, critiques, and suggestions (Johnson et al., 1991; Tsay & Brady, 2010). Although there may be need for students to work individually on the projects at some points, there must also be ample face-to-face interaction among group members. This provides opportunity for students to learn from each other, ask questions about content and strategy, and check for group understanding.

Finally, each member of a cooperative learning group must be encouraged to understand that the success or failure of the group depends on every member and that the entire group deals with consequences if one member does not actively work toward the achievement of the group goal (Johnson et al., 1991). For this reason, many cooperative learning procedures include a form of individual accountability where group members have a system for ensuring that everyone does his or her share of the work. Of course, one way to increase the feeling of accountability is to keep groups smaller. The smaller the group, the more responsible for the end product each group member is likely to feel.

> *Each student must be encouraged to understand that the success or failure of the group depends on every member and that the entire group deals with consequences if one member does not actively work toward the achievement of the group goal.*

An integral part of successful cooperative learning groups is the integration of interpersonal skills (Johnson et al., 1991; Tsay & Brady, 2010). Teachers must take time to teach conflict-management strategies, decision-making strategies, and effective communication skills. These are important skills for lifelong learning and students will benefit from practicing them in a safe cooperative learning group.

Students should also be taught to reflect on their group processes and discuss needed changes (Johnson et al., 1991, 2007). During the group activity, the teacher must provide time for group members to discuss behaviors that may need changing and behaviors that are profitable for the group. During group processing times, students can discuss what members are doing that is helpful or not helpful, as well as reflect on progress made toward the overall goal. The time allotted for group processing helps the group maintain effective working relationships.

A Jigsaw Cooperative Learning Example

Perhaps an example will help illustrate these concepts. One of the initial cooperative learning approaches described was the Jigsaw approach (Adams & Hamm, 1994; Johnson, Johnson, & Smith, 1999; Johnson et al., 2007). In this cooperative learning tactic, groups of students are created and only part of the content is provided to each participant; thus, the Jigsaw groups are viewed as teams of "experts" that must fit together the information like a jigsaw to create complete understanding of the topic for each student.

> *In a Jigsaw, groups of students are created and only part of the content is provided to each participant so teams must fit together the information like a jigsaw to create complete understanding of the topic for each student.*

Box 4.4   **Jigsaw Cooperative Learning Activity**

Second-Grade Classroom

North Carolina Standard Course of Study Objective 1.01—Describe the life cycle of animals including birth, developing into an adult, reproducing, aging, and death.

Students have been introduced to the study of life cycles. They have discussed various animal life cycles, including frogs, birds, and mealworms. For this particular portion, students will use the jigsaw cooperative learning strategy to research the butterfly life cycle.

- Each student will be assigned a particular stage of the butterfly life cycle, including egg, caterpillar, chrysalis, and cocoon.
- Students will join the others in the class who have their same life cycle resulting in four "expert" groups. Each expert group will be given one to two class periods to research their particular life stage, recording as many facts as possible. At the end of the research time, students will create a "final copy" paper that includes at least five sentences about their life cycle stage.
- During the next class period, students will remain in their expert groups and will create a craft depiction of their life cycle stage as follows:

  ○ Egg—paint a single section of a cardboard egg carton and tape/glue it onto a colored leaf cutout.

  ○ Caterpillar—paint three paper plates to create the body. Use pipe cleaners to create antennas.

  ○ Chrysalis—paint a paper towel holder brown/green to simulate a hanging chrysalis.

  ○ Butterfly—have students use washable markers to color an entire coffee filter as brightly as possible. Use a spray bottle when finished to lightly mist the coffee filter creating a tie-dye effect. When dry, use a pipe cleaner to scrunch the coffee filter up in the middle and tie it off creating two wings and antennas.

- During the final class period, take one "expert" from each group to create a jigsaw team including one egg expert, one caterpillar expert, one chrysalis expert, and one butterfly expert. Have students share their findings and depiction with their jigsaw team and allow class members to ask questions. Hang student life cycles together with their jigsaw team depicting the entire butterfly life cycle.

For example, if the class is learning about the life cycle of a frog, cooperative learning groups would be formed with roughly equal numbers of students in each group. Some teachers allow some student choice in formation of the groups, while other teachers designate group membership prior to beginning the activity. Typically, three to five cooperative groups may be formed in a given classroom. Next, within each group, individual students would be selected as "experts" on a specific subtopic dealing with frogs. Those experts from the various cooperative learning jigsaw groups would initially work together as "expert teams" working with other experts who are studying the same subtopic on the life cycle of a frog. For example, one expert team would learn about the egg mass; another expert team would study the tadpole, another would study the tadpole with legs, another the froglet, and another the mature adult frog. Once each expert team gathered all of their information, the original jigsaw groups would be reformed so that each expert could instruct their entire jigsaw team on his or her specialty area. The cooperative learning jigsaw team would then use the information from each expert to put together a complete presentation on the life cycle of a frog. Interdependence and cooperation is fostered because each expert is essential to the group. A sample jigsaw lesson plan is presented for a second-grade classroom in Box 4.4.

How Do I Implement Cooperative Learning?

Teachers, of course, will play a pivotal role in whether or not cooperative learning groups will be successful in the classroom. To provide a safe structured environment in which learning can occur, teachers must decide what content is to be learned, how many students will be in each cooperative learning group, the "expert" roles students should play in the group, as well as what resources and materials will be needed (Johnson et al., 1991, 2007; Johnson & Johnson, 1999). Once the cooperative learning groups have been formed, teachers will need to explicitly walk through the task each group is to perform and explain the desired outcome (Johnson & Johnson, 1999). It may be most helpful for the teacher to create a group rubric that delineates the group goal and the interdependence of each expert member of the group (Johnson & Johnson, 1999). Once groups are assigned and the task is explained, the teacher must continually monitor and assess student work. It is the teacher's job to ensure that students are completing the task accurately, effectively working together, and using appropriate interpersonal skills (Johnson & Johnson, 1999).

It may be helpful for teachers and students to work together to establish group norms, which specify the level of detail that must be mastered by each expert and then presented back to the cooperative learning team (Adams & Hamm, 1994; Johnson et al., 2007; Johnson & Johnson, 1999; Tsay & Brady, 2010). By brainstorming a set of specific group norms, students are given clear expectations about what is and what is not acceptable in the group. Also, such group norms provide a very appropriate peer pressure for each student to perform his or her role as expert. Norms allow for clearer communication during group processing as students are able to use specifics when discussing their own behavior and the behavior of their peers. Norms might include things such as the following:

- Group members will actively participate in group conversation.
- Group members will identify three main concepts and two specific details for each concept, and share those in written or verbal form with the group.
- Group members will make decisions as a team.
- Group members will value all opinions and respect each other's ideas.

To train students in the use of norms and group processing, teachers may opt to hold a "fishbowl" lesson. In this type of mini-lesson, a practice team would be given a problem and would role play solving the problem in a cooperative learning group (Johnson & Johnson, 1999). In such a "fishbowl," the teacher can have certain students to appear off task, present varying opinions, or inappropriately take control of the discussion. The class could then observe how the problems were handled by the other group members and discuss pros and cons of the group behavior. This would allow for concrete representation of how groups are to handle conflict and work together.

Other Cooperative Learning Procedures

Cooperative learning groups can take on many forms and can be used in any content area at virtually any grade level, and the following ideas are recommended for virtually any classroom. The procedure selected is up to the individual teacher, but all will increase the opportunities for students to collaboratively master their content, and thus all of these are quite social in nature.

The Three-Step Interview

The Three-Step Interview is a cooperative learning strategy that is particularly useful for situations where students are getting to know their group members (Adams & Hamm, 1994; Johnson et al., 1991, 2007; Johnson & Johnson, 1999; Tsay & Brady, 2010). When introducing and forming cooperative learning groups in the classroom, teachers can employ this strategy to help build interpersonal skills and group trust. Initially, teachers assign pairs of students to interview each other. The first student interviews his or her partner, and then the roles reverse and the interviewee becomes the interviewer. Once each partner has had a turn at each role, the pairs are then joined with another pair of students to form a group of four. Each person takes a turn introducing his or her partner and sharing the most interesting aspects of their interview.

Think-Pair-Share

Think-Pair-Share is a cooperative learning strategy that incorporates individual, partner, and large-group work (Adams & Hamm, 1994; Johnson et al., 1991, 2007; Johnson & Johnson, 1999). To use the strategy, teachers pose a particular question or problem to the class as a whole. Each student is required to think individually for a specified amount of time to formulate a personal opinion or solution. Students are then put into pairs where they share with each other their own answers to the posed problem.

> *Think-Pair-Share is a cooperative learning strategy that incorporates individual, partner, and large-group work.*

The Share step provides opportunity for students to articulate their ideas and listen to the ideas of others. This step is particularly important because it allows time for students to construct their meaning, reflect on their knowledge, and synthesize their information with the information of their partners. Finally, the pairs are called on to share their findings with a larger group (this can be several pairs placed together in groups of four to six students or can be the whole class). Some teachers also prefer to have students record their discoveries throughout the cooperative learning activity. Providing a Think-Pair-Share template such as the one in Box 4.5 helps students process their own thoughts, ensures accountability, and provides documentation for the teacher.

Send-a-Problem

Send-a-Problem is a cooperative learning strategy that encourages group interdependence and uses higher-order thinking skills, including synthesis and evaluation (Johnson et al., 2007; Johnson & Johnson, 1999). To implement this strategy, the teacher creates an authentic problem for the class to solve. To increase student motivation, teachers should prepare problems where connections between content and real-world applications are apparent for students.

Once a problem has been generated, it is clipped to the outside of a folder and passed to the first cooperative learning group. The group reads the problem and brainstorms as many possible solutions as they can generate in the specified amount of time. At the end of the specified time, the solutions are placed inside the folder and the entire folder is passed to the next group. The second cooperative learning group receives the folder, reads the problem, and again generates as many solutions as possible without looking at the first group's suggestions. Finally, the third cooperative learning team receives the folder, reads the problem, and reads the solutions proposed by the first two teams. It is the final group's responsibility to review the solutions, add their own, and consolidate to create a final class solution.

Box 4.5   **Think-Pair-Share Recording Template**

Think

Record three ideas you had while "thinking" about your question.

1. _____

2. _____

3. _____

Pair

Talk about your ideas with your partner. Record any new ideas your partner shared.

1. _____

2. _____

3. _____

Share

With your partner, decide which idea discussed is most important and highlight it. You will share that with the larger group. You can record any ideas the group shares that you liked as well.

1. _____

2. _____
3. _____

What Are the Advantages of Cooperative Learning?

Cooperative learning has been commonly used since the 1980s, and research has shown this to be an effective instructional approach in a variety of grade levels (Johnson et al., 2007; Marzano, Pickering, & Pollock, 2001; Tsay & Brady, 2010; Wachanga & Mwangi, 2004). In cooperative learning groups, students are able to interact and construct meaning as they explain new concepts and content to their peers (Adams & Hamm, 1994; Tsay & Brady, 2010). The interaction that takes place during cooperative learning activities forces students to synthesize their own information for the presentation to their peers while at the same time evaluating the information they are receiving (Tsay & Brady, 2010). This interaction works to create students who are able to see past their own opinions, listen with open minds, and value diversity in society. Due to the interdependence of the group, students often work harder than they might individually because they understand that the success of the group depends on every individual member.

> *Cooperative learning has been commonly used since the 1980s, and research has shown this to be an effective instructional approach in a variety of grade levels.*

The use of cooperative learning groups in the classroom also reaps important benefits in academic achievement (Johnson et al., 2007; Tsay & Brady, 2010; Wachanga & Mwangi, 2004). Studies in higher education show that students who used cooperative learning techniques performed significantly better than students who were not exposed to such innovative instructional strategies (Johnson et al., 2007; Wachanga & Mwangi, 2004). When students are given adequate amounts of time to understand the characteristics of cooperative learning groups, they are able to achieve higher levels of productivity (Wachanga & Mwangi, 2004). These higher levels of achievement and productivity are possibly by-products of the interdependence among group members. Lower-level students needing remediation and intervention learn through the interaction and support of their higher-level peers. The higher-level peers reap benefits because they are working through the material as they synthesize it for their group members (Wachanga & Mwangi, 2004).

Essentially, cooperative learning encourages students to take a hands-on approach to learning. Research shows gains of as much as 28 percent in students who were placed in cooperative learning groups (Marzano et al., 2001). In cooperative learning groups, students not only become familiar with the new content but also learn important skills for the 21st century as they work together with peers of varying backgrounds, academic levels, and cultural attitudes. Learners are actively participating with the material while they celebrate the diversity of their group. Students in cooperative learning groups are invested in their own learning as they seek answers to the problem given. For all of these reasons, this instructional approach is well suited for 21st-century instruction.

PEER TUTORING

What Is Peer Tutoring?

Peer tutoring is another instructional strategy that involves students in collaboratively learning the content, and many educators have recommended peer tutoring as an innovative instructional strategy for Tier 1

RTI instruction in general education (Harper & Maheady, 2007; Kroeger & Kouche, 2006). Peer tutoring pairs students of varying academic levels together to work through new content, review and practice previously covered content, or solve assigned problems. Like the strategies discussed previously, peer tutoring facilitates collaborative instruction, though in this case, most of the collaboration takes place in pairs of students rather than in small groups. Peer tutoring is a structured strategy that does require planning and organization on the part of the teacher. Several styles of peer tutoring are described next, including Peer Assisted Learning Strategy (PALS), Classwide Peer Tutoring, and Classwide Student Tutoring Teams.

> *Peer tutoring pairs students of varying academic levels together to work through new content, review and practice previously covered content, or solve assigned problems.*

PALS: The Peer Assisted Learning Strategy

The Peer Assisted Learning Strategy, or PALS, is built on a reciprocal relationship between peers in which each student serves as both tutor and tutee (Fuch et al., 2001; Fuchs et al., 2008; Kroeger & Kouche, 2006). In more traditional peer-tutoring models, a higher-achieving student was often paired with a lower-achieving student, and while benefits often resulted for the lower-achieving student, these models rarely offers significant learning opportunities for the higher-achieving students (Gartner & Riessman, 1993). Thus, the creators of the PALS program insisted that the program must create situations where all students in the general education classrooms can tutor each other; creating an environment where all students are actively involved with tasks, and in which all students benefit academically. When everyone has the opportunity to teach and synthesize the new material, students are able to learn through teaching rather than learning through listening (Gartner & Riessman, 1993).

Also, a reciprocal tutoring approach fosters higher engagement among all students, since students are much more invested in the process, and all recognize that their work is supportive of the learning of other students (Kroeger & Kouche, 2006). According to research done on PALS, this reciprocal relationship ultimately enhances student motivation as it encourages all students to become active participants in the learning process (Kroeger & Kouche, 2006; Stevens & Slavin, 1995).

How Do I Implement PALS?

Implementation of the program in the classroom requires approximately thirty-five minutes three to four days a week for reading, and thirty minutes two times a week for math. PALS is not intended as a

Box 4.6 Teaching Tip: A Sample Peer-Tutoring Script for Adding or Subtracting Fractions With Like Denominators

What type of problem is this (addition or subtraction)?

1. Do the operation indicated in the problem (either addition or subtraction) using only the numerators, or the numbers on top in each fraction. That answer becomes your new numerator.

2. If the new numerator is smaller than the denominator, you have arrived at your answer. Use the new numerator as the numerator for your answer, and use as the denominator the same denominator as the others in the problem. Write down that answer and you have finished.

3. If the new numerator is bigger than the denominator, you have a "hidden" whole number that is hiding within your new numerator. Usually that "hidden" whole number is one, but it may be two or three. We have to find that hidden number.

4. To see what that hidden whole number is, you find out how many times you can subtract the denominator from the new numerator. The number of times you can do that is your hidden whole number.

5. Write that hidden number as a whole number in the answer.

6. Then write down the remaining numerator as the numerator for your fraction in the answer, and use the same denominator for your answer! You are now finished.

core curriculum but rather as a supplemental curriculum, making it very appropriate for Tier 2 or Tier 3 instruction in an RTI framework. Prior to beginning, teachers need to explain the PALS procedures to their students.

The PALS teacher manual comes with scripted training lessons to help prepare students for their tutoring relationship. The program uses scripted lessons to guide the tutoring process, and each of those lessons presents present systematic, explicit instruction with clear models and various examples (Fuchs et al., 2001; Kroeger & Kouche, 2006). The scripted lesson is read by the coach while the tutee works on the problem. The coach is available and ready with adequate resources to provide additional help if needed. If a mistake is made, the coach calls that mistake to the attention of the tutee and encourages the tutee to rework the problem. A sample of this type of scripted lesson is provided in Box 4.6. (See page 123.)

Training is required for five days for students prior to undertaking this tutoring approach. In that training time students learn how to be both a tutor, referred to as a *coach*, and a tutee, referred to as a *player*. Students earn points during this training for correct coaching, which includes reading the scripted lessons correctly, helping the player figure out where mistakes are, and staying on task. The teacher manual also has scripts for each reading and math lesson. Once teachers go over the material with the students, students are able to complete their tutoring assignments with their partner (Fuchs et al., 2001).

> *The PALS program uses scripted lessons to guide the tutoring process, and each of those lessons presents present systematic, explicit instruction with clear models and various examples.*

During each tutoring session, students change roles, thereby sharing the role of coach and tutee. For example, in a typical PALS reading lesson, the partners take turns reading aloud with one person being the coach at a time. After the partner reading activity, students complete a retell, paragraph shrinking, and predication relay activities. The coach keeps track of the points earned, and these points go toward a reward for the student pair on a collaborative basis.

The PALS procedure is designed to support students in practice of material. Typically, a lead teacher will initially teach the lesson and skills required to the entire class. However, instead of having students complete individual practice problems, students worked through their PALS procedure to coach each other on the content using the scripted lesson. As students work with their PALS partner, the teacher visits each pair, monitoring and assisting the students as needed. Research continues to prove the efficacy of this innovate instructional strategy, with two primary results: there is increased engagement with content, and students' attitudes toward their work often shows dramatic improvement (Kroeger & Kouche, 2006).

PALS is designed as a supplement to existing reading and math curriculum, rather than as a replacement curriculum, and implementation of PALS is fairly inexpensive (Kroeger & Kouche, 2006). Teachers must have a teacher manual, blank transparencies, overhead projector, pocket folders for each student pair, and access to a photocopier. PALS also recommends using a kitchen timer to help pace the lesson. PALS math has worksheets designed to specifically target basic skills needed in each grade level. PALS reading for kindergarten and first grade also have a set of seventy student-lesson sheets. PALS does not provide reading material for Grades 2–6, so teachers in those grade levels are required to select appropriate passages for partner reading. Teachers must also complete prior assessments so that they understand the ability level of all students in the classroom. Data from assessments are used to make appropriate partner pairs. It is important to note that these partner pairs may need to change throughout the year based on student growth and strength and weaknesses noticed as the PALS program continues.

Classwide Peer Tutoring

Another way to use peer tutoring is through the implementation of a Classwide Peer Tutoring (CWPT) system. Unlike the PALS system, this is not a supplemental curriculum but rather an instructional procedure. CWPT is based on a team tutoring approach as opposed to pair reciprocal tutoring. Research shows that students are learning more in less time with CWPT as compared to conventional teacher-directed instruction (Topping & Elhy, 1998). Positive outcomes from the use of CWPT have been documented and replicated showing efficacy in reading, spelling, vocabulary, and math (Topping & Elhy, 1998). CWPT includes tutor and learner roles, both verbal and written practice of skills, verbal praise, points awarded for correct responses and appropriate participation, and the announcement of winning teams (Kamps, Barbetta, Leonard, & Delquardi, 1994). It is similar to PALS in that all students have a turn at being the tutor and at being the tutee.

How Do I Implement CWPT?

In this system, the class is divided into two teams, and then pairs of students are formed within those two teams (What Works Clearinghouse, 2010). Students may be paired randomly, by ability (either equally or adjacent skill levels), or by language proficiency depending on instructional goals for the lesson. As with PALS and other peer-tutoring approaches, the new content is initially taught by the classroom teacher. CWPT is typically implemented with existing curriculum materials and therefore can be adapted to fit any grade level or subject content (What Works Clearinghouse, 2010). Once new material is covered, students are directed to work in their pairs and interact with each other. This time in partners takes the place of independent seatwork that traditionally follows the introduction of new content (Harper & Maheady, 2007).

During the partner time, the tutor presents problems to the tutee and awards points for the tutee's performance. The roles are switched during each tutoring session—providing ample time for students to interact with the content. At the end of the tutoring session, points for each student are posted publicly and then added together to get a total team score. The entire session typically takes thirty minutes, with ten minutes for each student to tutor and five to ten minutes at the end for tallying points

(Harper & Maheady, 2007). Teachers typically change the content being studied, the teams, and the tutoring pairs on a weekly basis.

Both experimental and case study research has shown that CWPT is an effective instructional strategy for increasing academic achievement (Kamps et al., 1994; What Works Clearinghouse, 2010). However, studies performed also show that CWPT may increase social interactions for students with disabilities and for their nondisabled peers (Kamps et al., 1994; What Works Clearinghouse, 2010). In their study, students were given uninterrupted free time following the tutoring sessions, and the duration of social engagement also increased (Kamps et al., 1994), showing that CWPT helps to create a comfortable classroom environment—an environment where students feel safe to learn by listening and to learn by teaching.

> *Both experimental and case study research has shown that CWPT is an effective instructional strategy for increasing academic achievement.*

Classwide Student Tutoring Teams

Initially developed by Greenwood and his associates (Greenwood, Delquadri, & Carta, 1997; Harper & Maheady, 2007), Classwide Student Tutoring Teams (CSTT) are similar to PALS and CWPT, the only difference being that students work in instructional teams the entire time as opposed to pairs of students. The idea of instructional teams typically appeals to students in higher grades, making this instructional strategy particularly appropriate for middle and high school students (Harper & Maheady, 2007). Like the tutoring systems described previously, CSTT is reciprocal and each student takes a turn at being the tutor.

How Do I Implement CSTT?

Teachers interested in implementing CSTT in their classroom can obtain a video and a manual which will guide them through the implementation process (Harper, Maheady, Mallette, & Sacca, 1992). Just as with the other two aforementioned systems, the teacher teaches the new instructional content first and then provides the students a chance to interact with each other in two or more thirty-minute sessions each week (Harper & Maheady, 2007). When first implemented, the class is divided into groups of three or four students, including one high-performing student, one average student, and one low-performing student (Harper & Maheady, 2007). Once the students are placed in instructional teams, they should remain with this same group of students for a four- to six-week grading period unless the instructor notices a significant disparity develop (Harper & Maheady, 2007). During this time, students are encouraged to take pride in their team by naming themselves, decorating work folders, and taking ownership of group progress.

Once teams are established, it is the responsibility of each team member to ensure that everyone is learning the new content each week. Teachers who implement CSTT should develop study guides to accompany new content introduced each week. Each study guide should have anywhere from ten to thirty questions and answers pertaining to the new content (Harper et al., 1992; Harper & Maheady, 2007). Once the initial instruction has been given to the entire class, the team works together on the accompanying study guide. A sample method for having students work through the study guide in their CSTT teams is given in Box 4.7.

What Are the Advantages of Peer Tutoring?

A growing body of research over the last two decades details the effectiveness of peer tutoring in varying grade levels (Fuchs et al., 2008; Harper et al., 1992; Harper & Maheady, 2007; McDuffie, Mastropieri, & Scruggs, 2009; Wood et al., 2007). Peer tutoring works because it promotes student enjoyment while increasing students' on-task time. Students who are able to work with their peers to study content experience less boredom that comes from doing rote practice and worksheets, and the research suggests that there are benefits for all parties involved in the tutoring situation. Students using peer tutoring increased their levels in oral and silent reading, writing, discussion of academic content, and on-task behavior (Topping & Elhy, 1998). In one study of CWPT, students in urban schools performed significantly better when participating in peer tutoring than comparison group on summative reading, math, and language tests (Greenwood, Delquardi, & Hall, 1989).

To ensure that both the tutor and the tutee receive these benefits, careful planning on the part of the teacher must take place. Teachers must take time to train the students on how to be both a tutor and a tutee; provide highly structured activities with appropriate materials and resources; and continually monitor and provide feedback (Steedly, Dragoo, Arefeh, & Luke, 2008). This extra work is well worth it for teachers as well. Peer tutoring improves student retention of content material, promotes a deeper understanding of the content that enables teachers to set higher academic goals, and provides a cost- and time-effective way to provide differentiated instruction (National Tutoring Association, n.d.).

CONCLUSIONS

The synthesis of RTI, technology, and differentiated instruction will characterize classrooms of the 21st century, and as that synthesis increasingly takes effect, educators should anticipate significant changes in instructional procedures. While complete delineation of these anticipated changes is not possible, there are some tentative conclusions that can be drawn on what these changes might entail. Clearly, increased use of technology will

> **Box 4.7** **Teaching Tip: CSTT Peer-Tutoring Activity Directions**
>
> 1. To begin the CSTT team activity, one student selects the first card from the deck, and the number on that card indicates the question number on the study guide that will be addressed.
>
> 2. The student seated to the left of the card selector is designated the "tutor" for that question, and that tutor reads the designated question to his or her teammates.
>
> 3. Each of the teammates then writes his or her answer to that question down and shows their responses to the tutor, who checks them against the answers on the study guide.
>
> 4. If the answer is correct, tutors award the students five points. If an answer is incorrect, the tutor shares the correct answer with the teammate who answered incorrectly, and requires that student to write the correct answer to the question two or three times.
>
> 5. That student is then awarded two points by the tutor. No points are given to students who refuse to cooperate with the tutor or do not correct their mistakes.
>
> 6. After points are assigned for each teammate, the next teammate on the left becomes the new tutor, and the teammate to his or her left draws another card.
>
> 7. Students continue through the study guide, and through the deck, as many times as possible, repeating study guide questions, as possible, if they finish the entire deck. This allows them to earn more points. Teachers are encouraged to review Harper and Maheady (2007) for additional information on implementation of CSTT.

characterize classrooms of the future, and that technology will represent more than merely an informational delivery system; rather, it will provide opportunities for active, engaged learners to create knowledge and content that is then published worldwide.

Next, while a considerable amount of instruction will, in all likelihood, be computerized, there will also be an increased need for collaborative instructional procedures that involve groups of students. As noted previously, such collaborative procedures more closely resemble real-world tasks that will be required of students in the 21st century (Partnership for 21st Century Skills, 2004, 2009c).

PBL, cooperative instruction, and peer tutoring programs such as PALS, CWPT, and CSTT all provide opportunities for collaborative instruction, and one might anticipate increased use of these instructional procedures over the next decade. All of these instructional methods effectively replace worksheets with engaging student activities that promote increased on-task time with content. As the research described previously has repeatedly demonstrated, these innovative instructional strategies increase student engagement and result in higher levels of learning (Harper & Maheady, 2007). In line with the RTI, technology, and differentiated instruction synthesis, these instructional procedures are likely to characterize virtually every classroom in the near future, and educators are well advised to begin now the implementation of these practices, if they have not already done so.

5 The Teaching/ Learning Revolution

Preparing for Systems Change

PLANNING FOR THE CHANGES

It is extremely difficult to offer advice on how school faculties might prepare for the changes that this dynamic synthesis is likely to bring about. First, one harsh reality is that increased technology in the classroom costs money, and some schools are much more limited in expendable funds than are others. Some classrooms already have a computer on every desk, whereas instructional computers are rare in other classrooms, and as this book is written in 2011, the latter type of classroom is probably closer to the norm. With that noted, the quickly developing iPad and notebook technology may assist schools in the near future by making Internet connectivity a desktop option, and those devices tend to be less expensive than laptop computers. Still, increased technology for our classrooms will cost money, and while RTI and implementation of differentiated instruction are not typically associated with large budgetary expenditures, the increased use of technology is.

Next, the synthesis of these factors, which is the primary thesis of this book, suggests that each of these factors impacts the other in profound ways; of course, such impact holds implications for implementation. For example, a school's access to technology will impact not only teachers' use of technology-based instruction but also how these other changes are implemented. Schools with access to increased technology and software are likely to undertake a different implementation plan for RTI than schools with less access to technology. For example, schools that choose to use AIMSweb for progress monitoring in Tiers 2 and 3 will implement RTI differently than schools who use paper-and-pencil measures of reading and mathematics progress, which they might glean from the Internet at no costs (e.g., on the website www.easy.cbm). Schools that implement computer-driven interventions in the various tiers will have another set of progress monitoring tools for their RTI efforts.

> *A school's access to technology will impact not only technology-based instruction but also how RTI and differentiated instruction are implemented as well.*

Because RTI is the most prominent of the nationally pressing issues in 2011 as this book was written, we present some initial suggestions for planning the implementation of RTI. These focus on schools where technology and technology budgets might be quite limited, but this plan may also be used by schools that can afford some of the technology supports for differentiated instruction in the classroom or for RTI implementation. Later in this chapter, we present some guidance and several tools that can be used by school faculty to consider implementation of technology, RTI, and differentiated instruction together.

MOVING INTO RESPONSE TO INTERVENTION

As a first step toward implementation of RTI, many proponents of RTI have recommended that schools should create a school leadership team, a professional learning community (PLC), or a schoolwide RTI task force—a group of professionals dedicated to planning the schoolwide implementation effort over a three- to five-year period (Bender, 2009a; DuFour, DuFour, & Eaker, 2008; DuFour, DuFour, Eaker, & Many, 2006). Such PLCs have been shown to be quite effective in making substantive change in instructional practices, including everything from RTI, differentiating instruction, and implementation of increased use of technology at the school level (DuFour et al., 2006; DuFour et al., 2008; Johnson & Smith, 2008).

> *Schools should use or create a professional learning community (PLC) dedicated to planning the schoolwide RTI implementation effort, as a major focus in their school reform or school-improvement planning.*

An initial task for that group might be to explore the RTI resources that are available on the Internet. For example, the National Center for Response to Intervention (www.rti4success.org) presents a great deal of information on RTI in various situations across the grade levels. Other websites, such as the site for the RTI Action Network, also present useful information to guide RTI implementation (www.rtinetwork.org). Box 5.1 presents more information on these sites, and several additional websites for educators to review as they begin or continue their efforts toward full RTI implementation. These sites tend to emphasize the skill areas of reading and mathematics, along with improved behavior, and as shown previously in Chapter 1, nearly all RTI efforts nationally have been directed toward these areas.

Box 5.1 **RTI Informational Websites**

RTI Action Network

http://www.rtinetwork.org/

The **RTI Action Network** is dedicated to effective implementation of RTI. It was created by the National Council of Learning Disabilities and contains a variety of free resources for schools including webcasts, national online forums, implementation guidelines, and research summaries. Visitors can also sign up to receive a newsletter, and every school should have several PLC members register for that free service.

IES What Works Clearinghouse

http://ies.ed.gov/ncee/wwc/publications

This clearinghouse is supported by the federal government and provides research syntheses on various instructional programs that may be used either in differentiating instruction or in various tiers of RTI. Evaluations of the scientific support of these curricula are provided, but the standards for research on this site are quite rigorous, and if a particular curriculum is not evaluated here, the reader should attempt to find that curriculum on other websites.

Easy CBM

http://www.easycbm.com

This website provides access to various curriculum-based measures in reading and mathematics for the K–8 grade levels. Mathematics measures are keyed to the focal points identified by the National Council of Teachers of Mathematics, and benchmark scoring is provided for the reading assessments.

University of Oregon Website

http://oregonreadingfirst.uoregon.edu

This site provides information on supplemental curricula that might be used Tier 2 or Tier 3 interventions in RTI.

(Continued)

(Box 5.1 Continued)

National Center on Response to Intervention

http://www.rti4success.org/

The National Center on RTI is a helpful site that provides fact sheets, presentations, training modules on RTI, and various issues within RTI. This location adds resources frequently. Here also, practitioners sign up to receive an online monthly newsletter.

Center on Positive Behavioral Interventions and Supports (PBIS) http://www.pbis.org/

This is a federally funded, National Technical Assistance Center on behavioral interventions, many of which can be used within the RTI framework. It was established to foster the discipline systems needed for successful learning and social development of students. Positive Behavior Support (PBS) aims to prevent inappropriate behavior through teaching and reinforcing appropriate behavior and social skills.

There are several issues and questions that arise whenever a school undertakes planning for RTI, and these have been presented and described fairly extensively elsewhere in the RTI literature (Bender, 2009a; Buffum, Mattos, & Weber, 2009). All of these must be discussed by school faculty at some point. A list of these issues and questions is presented in Box 5.2, and the PLC of the school should identify guidelines from their district or state that addresses these questions and, from that basis, undertake discussions to make decisions on these questions.

Box 5.2   Discussion Questions and Issues on RTI Implementation

The PLC or administrators can use these questions as a basis for discussions in the group or with the faculty at large. All tentative decisions should be noted and reconsidered at least once by the group prior to implementation.

1. What is the best way to make certain that all students are provided the support they need to succeed in reading, mathematics, and behavior? Are additional interventions necessary for some students? Who should deliver those interventions?

   _____

   _____

   _____

2. What academic and behavioral support programs are currently in place in our school in reading, mathematics, and behavior that might serve or be adapted to serve as Tier 2 or Tier 3 interventions?

_____

_____

_____

3. Are there support instructional personnel (e.g., math coaches, reading specialists, special education inclusion teachers) in our school that could help make Tier 2 and Tier 3 interventions available? Please explain.

_____

_____

_____

4. Are there currently various hardcopy or computer programs that would be appropriate supplemental curricula for Tier 2 and Tier 3 interventions at our school?

_____

_____

_____

5. How will our school manage the concept of universal screening to identify students with academic or behavioral needs that are not currently being met? Do we administer specific assessment tools three times yearly or use existing screening measures?

_____

_____

_____

6. What will be our standard for describing the intensity of Tier 2 and Tier 3 interventions? How many minutes per day, days per week, for how many weeks are necessary?

_____

_____

_____

7. What pupil-to-teacher ratio will we require for these intensive interventions at the Tier 2 and Tier 3 levels?

_____

_____

_____

(Continued)

(Box 5.2 Continued)

8. When should teachers approach the student support team in the RTI process (prior to initiation of a Tier 2 intervention, or after such intervention is completed and a data chart summarizing the intervention efficacy is available)?

_____

_____

_____

9. What professional development is necessary to facilitate RTI (e.g., mathematics interventions for Tier 2 or Tier 3, assessment tools in various areas for particular grade levels)?

_____

_____

_____

10. Who can serve on the PLC and do further planning for RTI in our school? What tasks are various faculty willing to undertake?

_____

_____

_____

Another task for the PLC might be to develop an ongoing timeline for RTI implementation. As schools move into RTI, many issues will arise that impact all students in the RTI process, as well as all teachers in the school. RTI implementation will be a multiyear process (Bender, 2009a; Deshler, 2010; Duffy, 2007; Gibbs, 2009), and an overall plan for that type of multiyear process is another task that the PLC should undertake. Planning professional development activities, mentoring teachers, and other tactics to facilitate implementation over a two- or three-year period is recommended (Bender, 2009a). An example of such a planning process is presented in Box 5.3, and educators should feel free to use that set of activities as points to consider, but they should also modify them in ways that make it specific for their situation. For example, some schools have RTI in reading well in hand and merely need to expand their efforts to include mathematics or behavior, and this planning document should be adjusted accordingly.

| Box 5.3 | Activities for a PLC Focused on RTI |

RTI Goals for Tidioute Charter School, Tidioute, PA: 2013–2014.

Academic Year: 2013–2014

1. All teachers will receive a minimum of four hours of inservice on each topic below:
   (a) RTI procedures in PA—the first inservice on RTI planning will be completed during the first month of school, and an outside expert (perhaps from the state Department of Education) will be used to introduce RTI to our faculty, and discuss model RTI programs in PA
   (b) Various screening assessments and procedures for performance monitoring in reading and mathematics
   (c) Computerized reading and mathematics interventions available in our county schools in reading, math, and Algebra I or Algebra Recovery

2. Members of the PLC for RTI will meet monthly and undertake various book studies and web reviews on model RTI programs in high schools and middle schools around the nation.

3. During the second meeting during this academic year, the PLC will select specific professional development opportunities at various state and national conferences, and identify various PLC members to attend these meetings. The goal will be for those PLC members to attend these conferences and bring back additional information on RTI implementation to share with the faculty in the next scheduled faculty meeting. These will be done in a thirty-minute presentation to the entire faculty.

4. The PLC for RTI will develop and present an RTI implementation plan for RTI implementation in reading, mathematics, and behavior for all grade levels to the school faculty. It will be discussed at one meeting, modified as suggested, and adopted at the next meeting. Current recommendations for the RTI implementation timeline are presented herein.

5. The PLC for RTI will work with the principal on necessary resources for RTI on an ongoing basis. These may include
   (a) additional professional or support staff for RTI interventions;
   (b) purchase of intervention curricula in various areas; and
   (c) discussions of reallocations of job responsibilities for RTI implementation.

(Continued)

(Box 5.3 Continued)

6. The PLC for RTI will implement a needs assessment on RTI among the faculty.

7. The PLC for RTI will conduct a school-based inventory to identify assessments, curricula, and specialized staff training currently available at the schools that may assist in RTI implementation.

8. Items on the schoolwide planning grid will be discussed at the end of the year, to note any changes from the initial planning session.

9. Data on student referrals to special education and data on school dropouts will be collected at the end of this year as a comparison measure on efficacy of RTI.

RTI Goals for Academic Year 2014–2015

1. Tidioute Charter School will implement universal screening in reading and mathematics for all students twice each year. These screenings will be based on assessments chosen by the school faculty.

2. Tidioute Charter School will undertake screening for all students and identify students who are performing two or more years below grade level in reading or mathematics. Those students will be placed into intensive Tier 2 interventions.

3. Tidioute Charter School will provide Tier 2 interventions in behavior for all students requiring more intensive behavior problem management.

4. Tier 2 interventions in reading and mathematics will be defined as thirty minutes per day, a minimum of four days per week. This definition will be discussed and voted on by the faculty.

5. By January 2015, Tidioute Charter School will provide Tier 3 interventions in reading and mathematics for students requiring them. These will be provided five days per week for a minimum of forty minutes per day. These will be provided at the same time and in the same manner as the Tier 2 interventions.

6. The PLC for RTI at Tidioute Charter School will be expanded to include all former members as well as all department chairpersons.

7. Various teachers will be invited to attend professional development opportunities that address RTI implementation in reading, English, mathematics, and behavior.

8. The schoolwide planning grid will be used again at both schools in May of this and each subsequent year, specifically to note any changes from the initial planning session.

9. Data on student referrals to special education will be collected at the end of this and each subsequent year as a comparison measure on efficacy of RTI. These data will be compared to data from the previous year to determine the impact of RTI in our school.

RTI Goals for Academic Year 2015–2016

1. Tidioute Charter School will continue universal screening in mathematics and reading for all students, and will begin behavioral screening for all students in the fall of this year.

2. By January 2016, Tidioute Charter School will collect behavioral data on students recommended by teachers for supplemental behavioral interventions. Ultimately, one or more screening instruments in behavior will be identified and recommended to the school faculty by the PLC for RTI. Each school has previously implemented a schoolwide positive behavior supports system, and articulation of those efforts with the RTI process will be the focus of the PLC for RTI during the 2015–2016 academic year.

3. Data on student referrals to special education and student dropouts will be collected at the end of this year as a comparison measure on efficacy of RTI. These data will be compared to data from previous years to determine the impact of RTI in our school.

RTI implementation should be viewed as a multiyear process, and an overall plan for that type of multiyear process is another task that the PLC may wish to undertake.

PLANNING FOR THE DYNAMIC SYNTHESIS

Schools that have the capacity and the necessary funding to infuse more technology into their program as they implement RTI and differentiated instruction have additional options. As we have stated throughout this text, the three factors of RTI, technology, and differentiated instruction are currently merging in a dynamic synthesis that is reshaping and will continue to drastically reshape the teaching/learning process in schools.

This book represents the first effort to discuss this synthesis directly and indicate where these change agents may take the teaching/learning process over the next decade. We believe that, over the next decade, educators will initiate a more responsive, highly differentiated if not totally individualized instructional approach across the public school grade levels—an approach that makes maximum use of modern technologies, including some communications technologies and social-networking technologies that, as late as 2011, were not seen as instructional technologies.

Of course, we should point out that many teachers are already "there" in terms of implementing differentiated instruction, RTI, or the recent technological innovations in the classroom. This is particularly true in the elementary grades since RTI essentially began with a reading emphasis in those grade levels.

However, other teachers are not yet on board with all of these newly emerging instructional techniques, and still other teachers may be well versed on some of these innovations, but not in others. Nevertheless, this transition to a new, more dynamic, and individualized forms of instruction, rooted in the commitment of RTI, implementation of technology, and differentiated instruction across all classrooms, will take place regardless of who lags behind. Simply put, the broader environment in which schools exist simply demands these innovations. Thus, we believe that it is advisable to note the beginning of a new era in instruction, a revolution in teaching based on this dynamic synthesis.

While changes that are precipitated by the interaction of multiple factors are more difficult to predict than a singular change precipitated by only one cause, we do believe that RTI, technology, and differentiated instruction continue to create fundamental changes in teaching, and that these three catalysts for change have and will continue to have an impact that is much greater than the impact of each single factor in isolation. Of course, exactly how these changes may impact each other remains to be seen.

WHAT CAN BE PREDICTED ABOUT THIS DYNAMIC SYNTHESIS?

The last chapter presented several instructional models that have been identified as fitting nicely within the synthesis resulting from RTI, differentiated instruction, and increased technology in the schools. In that sense, it is reasonable to suggest that our instructional models will be modified as these instructional techniques—project-based learning, cooperative instruction, and peer tutoring—play an increasing role in our classrooms. However, other areas of education are likely to be impacted as well.

For example, the assessment process and school curricula have long been emphasized across the nation, and the educational standards movement has resulted in major efforts by school faculties to align their educational curriculum with statewide, high-stakes testing. However, as both technology and RTI initiatives come into play, both curriculum and assessment are sure to be areas impacted by this dynamic synthesis.

One can easily imagine the entire public school curriculum as a CD-based or web-based curriculum, without traditional texts. The PLATO Curriculum, discussed in Chapter 2, represents one such curriculum that is already available commercially, and thus, this curriculum represents one of the initial "imaginings" in the introduction to this book. These types of curricula are supported by practice activities online, enrichment activities, simulation activities, or project-based learning scenarios, and a host of other digital supports, as well as built-in assessments. Students might, in that context, complete many if not most of their instructional activities on the computer online, and the software would then score the students and note for the teacher each student's strengths and weaknesses. Again, this is possible today, and these types of curricula are used in exactly that fashion in various programs for dropouts or GED programs.

In such a technology-based educational environment, all levels of assessment will be built into the curriculum and managed by the software, including everything ranging from large-scale statewide, norm-referenced assessments to unit assessments used by the whole class, to daily or weekly progress monitoring RTI checks for students in Tier 2 or Tier 3 interventions. When educational curricular materials come with intensive assessment options built in, as do most online or CD-based computer programs today, what need will there be for large-scale expenditures for statewide assessments?

Imagine the curriculum as a CD-based or web-based curriculum, including all levels of assessment ranging from large-scale statewide assessments to daily or weekly progress monitoring RTI checks for students in Tier 2 or Tier 3 interventions within the online curriculum.

Thus, as technology and RTI increasingly impact each other, we might well witness the eventual merger of the instructional curriculum and assessment into one seamless whole, a curriculum and assessment package provided in digital format that students progress through at their own pace, with their learning monitoring and facilitated by their teacher. In such an online or CD-based instructional environment, the distinction between instruction and assessment becomes so blurred so as to be virtually meaningless. Further, such a curriculum would be almost totally differentiated in that each individual student would be receiving instruction targeted at exactly his or her learning level and adapted to address his or her learning preferences. Of course, educators may well debate the advantages or disadvantages of such a seamless curriculum/assessment program, and some might argue against such a seamless, digital instructional system for one reason or another. The point here is that such a curriculum resulting in the synthesis of RTI, technology, and differentiated instruction is not only possible but also already available to a degree, and has been implemented with positive effects, as shown in Chapter 2. Given the evidence for efficacy of such totally individualized curricula, is there any doubt that such curricula represents the future of education?

WHAT OTHER CHANGES MIGHT RESULT?

As the examples herein show, these three factors will create classrooms that look very different from traditional instruction. Our goal in this book is to help prepare all educators for that change, as well as prepare administrators, leadership teams, and PLCs to guide and facilitate those changes. While not every aspect of this anticipated transition can be foreseen, we can suggest at least two other changes that will make classrooms of the future look very different from classrooms of the past.

> *While not every aspect of this anticipated transition can be foreseen, we can suggest at least two changes that will make classrooms of the future look very different from classrooms of the past.*

First, as stated previously, these three catalysts for change should bring a significant decrease if not an outright end to whole-group instruction in most core classes. Students sitting in straight rows of desks, facing the front of the class, as teachers deliver information (e.g., lectures or discussions) will become a thing of the past because students in general education classes today are simply too diverse in their needs and learning approaches for a whole-group instruction to work very well over the long term. In contrast, differentiation promotes wide diversity in instructional approaches (Bender, 2008), and while high-quality differentiated instruction is possible within the traditional whole-class framework, other models described herein, such as learning centers, simply make differentiated instruction much easier. Both RTI and technology now offer a means toward the end goal of differentiation to meet the needs of every student in the class, and we gladly anticipate the decrease or the virtual end of whole-group instruction in core content classes.

Next, we anticipate a changing role for teachers in this new dynamic educational environment: The teacher's role is likely to change from the role of instructional delivery agent to one of instructional facilitator, a teacher that carefully considers each student's individual needs and then pairs students with the software-based instruction or places them into small instructional groups for project-based learning tasks or cooperative instruction that exactly meets their instructional needs and learning styles.

Next, today's teachers and teachers in the future will spend much less time developing lesson plans. In point of fact, nearly every curriculum today provides prepared lesson plans in the instructor's manual, and while those typically follow the whole-group lesson plan outline described in Chapter 3, the fact is that these lesson plans have, for decades, been provided for teachers. Instead, teachers will spend much more time seeking out a wider variety of instructional information-delivery options, such as digital media presentations, collaborative small-group explorations, and project-based learning ideas. Then the teachers will spend their time facilitating such small-group instructional interactions centered on student-generated questions or student selection from among various projects.

> *The role of teacher will change from the role of instructional delivery agent to instructional facilitator.*

Finally, as the use of PBL increases over the next decade, the unit-based instructional basis for many elementary, middle, and secondary content classes will change rather drastically. Thus, differentiated instruction within a PBL framework is likely to change how classes operate, and with this catalogue of substantive changes in mind, it seems clear that we are looking at a whole new world in the teaching/learning process in the immediate future.

PLCS LEADING THE CHANGE!

With this dynamic synthesis already underway, educators can do much to anticipate and facilitate these changes. First, we caution educators not to dive into only one of these instructional innovations to the exclusion of the others since these three factors—RTI, technology, and differentiated instruction—are so mutually interdependent. We believe that professional development must involve systematic involvement of all three of these areas, and thus, we recommend a major school reform effort directed at each of these instructional innovations together. In fact, we believe it is virtually impossible to discuss any one of these factors in the absence of the others. Therefore, to begin implementation, we would suggest the following steps.

1. *Begin Immediately.* Using a PLC (DuFour, DuFour, Eaker, & Karhanek, 2004; DuFour et al., 2006; DuFour et al., 2008) or a school leadership team as the change agent, educators in every school should or continue to seek professionaldevelopment opportunities that stress all of these innovations. Regardless of where most of the school faculty may be regarding the implementation of these innovations, we suggest that educators begin immediately with a view toward moving faculty from where they are to full implementation of these dynamic

instructional practices. Again, RTI, technology-based instruction, and differentiated instruction represent teaching for the 21st century, and all educators should move in these directions.

2. *Plan for Comprehensive Differentiation in All Classes.* Differentiated instruction should be the basis for Tier 1 instruction in all core content areas as well as most other classes, and if that is not already true in a particular school, initial emphasis should be placed here. Effective differentiation will increase student achievement (Tomlinson, Brimijoin, & Navaez, 2008) and thus will decrease the number of students requiring a Tier 2 or Tier 3 intervention. For many schools, these changes demand that differentiated instruction be emphasized as a first step.

Further, by continuously stressing the importance of differentiation as the basis for all Tier 1 instruction, differentiated instruction becomes tied to the RTI process in a seamless educational support system for all students. This seamless instructional practice, providing assistance for all students in both general education classes and in Tiers 2 and 3 of the RTI pyramid, represents 21st-century education; this should be the goal for every educator, and differentiated instruction plays a critical role in that, which is why virtually every state with an RTI plan emphasized differentiated instruction at the Tier 1 level of the RTI endeavor (Berkeley et al., 2009).

3. *Plan for Long-Term, Multifactor Change.* Rather than independent efforts toward implementation of these initiatives, we again recommend a comprehensive, multiyear plan to encompass all of these innovations and thereby increase the schoolwide emphasis on this new dynamic synthesis. While workshops on all of these individual topics are widely available, finding workshops that undertake a discussion of all three of these catalysts for change is more difficult. In point of fact, how many authors, workshop providers, or other "experts" are really well versed in all three of these innovative changes? However, such comprehensive professional development opportunities are becoming more available, and having teachers empower themselves in these three areas together will lead to the growth in achievement we see for all students.

To illustrate this type of comprehensive, multiyear plan, a sample plan driven by the PLC is presented in Box 5.4. While similar to the RTI plan presented already, this planning instrument includes not only RTI but also technology and increased differentiated instruction as part of the planning process. Of course, all such professional development plans should be based on local needs and resources, and this sample merely represents the types of activities that such a comprehensive plan might entail.

| Box 5.4 | A Sample PLC Activities Plan for Martin Elementary Addressing the Dynamic Synthesis of RTI, Technology, and Differentiated Instruction |

Activities for Academic Year 2012–2013

1. The PLC will implement a needs assessment among the faculty on RTI, technology, and differentiated instruction in August of this year to develop information for the initial professional development planning.

2. The PLC working as a whole will conduct a school-based inventory to identify available technology options, currently used assessments and curricula, or specialized staff training at Martin Elementary that may assist in implementation of technology-based instruction, RTI, or differentiated instruction.

3. During this academic year, all teachers will receive three hours of inservice on each of the six targeted professional development areas. These professional development activities should be scheduled in the fall of 2012, in roughly the following order.
   a. RTI procedures for our state—in that meeting, the RTI planning grid will be introduced as our primary planning mechanism. This will be completed during the first month of school, and an outside expert (perhaps from the state department of education) will introduce RTI to our faculty
   b. The use of various screening assessments for performance monitoring in reading and mathematics
   c. Computerized curricula and interventions currently available in our county school in reading and math
   d. Differentiated instructional strategies in core areas of reading, mathematics, science, and history
   e. Use of webquests, whiteboards, and project-based learning, cooperative learning, and other strategies for differentiating instruction at the Tier 1 level
   f. Instructional strategies for using smartphones, Facebook, and other social media as teaching tools

4. In September 2012, members of the PLC will identify subcommittees of the PLC focused on RTI, technology, and differentiated instruction, and will agree to participate on one of those subcommittees.

(Continued)

(Box 5.4 Continued)

5. Each member of one of those subcommittees will select one or two specific professional development opportunities related to the topics above, involving participation in various state and national conferences during this academic year. Those members will attend these events. In each case, a thirty-minute workshop will be provided to the faculty by the PLC team member on the topic of the conference.

6. Those PLC members will initiate a book study of an appropriate professional development book on one of the six targeted areas by November 15, 2012. Each faculty member is expected to participate in one such book study from that date and throughout the spring of 2013. Book study groups will be expected to read the books and discuss during a minimum of three thirty-minute meetings. Each member of the book study group will then prepare a three-page plan for implementation of the strategy or ideas discussed in his or her class. Those will be presented both to the PLC and the principal's office.

7. The PLC subcommittee on RTI will develop and present an RTI implementation plan for RTI, with an emphasis on differentiated instruction in all core classes at the Tier 1 level by September 30, 2012. This group will initially plan for RTI implementation in reading and present that plan to the faculty. The plan will then be modified as necessary. This plan will be adopted at a subsequent meeting of the faculty in November 2012.

8. By January 2013, Martin Elementary will implement RTI in reading by providing differentiated reading instruction in all classes, and Tier 2 and Tier 3 interventions in reading, as needed.

9. Data on student referrals to special education for reading problems, and student referrals to the office for disciplinary reasons, will be collected by the school principal at the end of this year and compared to referrals from the previous year as a comparison measure on the efficacy of our efforts in RTI, differentiation in general education, and technology-based instruction.

Activities for Academic Year 2013–2014

1. Implementation of RTI in both mathematics and behavior will be the focus of the professional development activities this year, in conjunction with ongoing professional development in the six targeted areas from the 2012–2013 academic year. The goal will

be to complete implementation of RTI in reading, mathematics, and behavior by the end of 2014. Toward that end, the PLC will plan three-hour professional development activities in the following areas for the fall of 2013:

a. RTI for positive behavior supports (assessment of behavior problems, progress monitoring, and intervention ideas for Tier 2 behavioral interventions)

b. RTI in mathematics (screening instruments, progress monitoring instruments, curricula to be used in Tier 2 and Tier 3 mathematics interventions)

2. The PLC at Martin Elementary will determine what additional professional development activities should be presented in each of the six areas targeted in the previous academic year.

3. PLC members will initiate a second book study of an appropriate professional development book on one of the eight targeted areas listed for either 2012–2013 or 2013–2014. Each faculty member is expected to participate in one such book study, as described previously.

4. By January 2014, Martin Elementary will implement Tier 2 interventions in mathematics and behavior supports for all students requiring more intensive assistance in these areas.

5. By August 2014, Martin Elementary will plan to provide Tier 3 interventions in mathematics and behavior supports as needed by all students.

6. In May 2013, a schoolwide faculty meeting will be held to focus on the implementation efforts of RTI, technology-based instruction, and differentiation, and teachers will be invited to request specific, additional professional development assistance for the coming year.

4. *Reward Innovative Teaching!* While there may be some need for outside expertise in particular areas, we suggest that schools use "homegrown" expertise. Most schools currently have teachers who are experts in one or more of these initiatives. For example, virtually every administrator can identify one or several teachers who use technology in innovative ways, and those teachers should be not only rewarded but also showcased via informal (or formal, depending on the comfort level of those teachers) workshops for the rest of the faculty.

The school-based PLC should seek out the teachers within their own buildings who are practicing cutting-edge technology applications, well-researched RTI practices, or effective differentiated strategies. Having those teachers provide in-house workshops, facilitate book studies among the faculty, or coach/mentor other teachers can be some of the most effective professional development opportunities available. Certainly, teachers who have been successful in these areas are meeting the needs of all students in their classes more effectively and should serve as model teachers for others within the building or school district.

In this context, the Race to the Top initiative of President Obama (Clarke, 2010) provides the opportunity for merit pay incentives for master teachers. PLCs should seek out those teachers to facilitate in-house learning opportunities in these areas and then find ways to reward those master teachers as they move more in the directions of increased differentiation, implementation of rigorous RTI procedures, and teaching with research proven instructional technology.

5. *Make the Commitment of RTI.* Knowing the RTI pyramid and actually implementing RTI in a committed fashion across the school at all grade levels is quite different. Chapter 1 of this book opened with an explanation of RTI as a *commitment* on the part of teachers to provide whatever help and instructional support necessary to change a child's life. That commitment can be an effective basis for discussing RTI within a school faculty, and faculty tend to find that commitment as a worthy goal.

However, teachers will need much more than merely an informational presentation on RTI; they will need to understand the "why" of RTI and to see that it will positively impact the school's overall success in increasing schoolwide achievement. Again, a three- to five-year implementation period, with many discussions of RTI, coupled with efforts to constantly improve the schoolwide implementation of RTI will be necessary.

6. *Plan for Increased Technology.* This book has merely scratched the surface as far as the impact of technology in teaching is concerned. In fact, technology is likely to be the most important and impactful single factor leading to instructional changes in the next decade, and PLCs should plan and budget for enhanced technology in the schools.

In the simplest terms, we can no longer have schools lag behind industry or personal entertainment in our society as far as technology applications are concerned. As long as some teachers know less about technology or use technology less frequently than most students, our educational endeavors will suffer at the national level (Partnership for 21st Century Skills, 2007). At the school-district level, the basic technologies for effective instruction must be made available in every classroom, and strong support from school administrators, school faculty, and PLCs can be crucial in motivating school districts toward increasing use of technology.

Of course, it is neither advisable nor possible in most cases to merely purchase computers and software for all students in all classes. Rather, a long-term infusion of technology is advisable, providing technologies and professional development in combination, given the school's current budget constraints. Over time, all educators must be trained to use modern instructional technologies in their various subject areas, and such training is the key to effective use of various technology applications.

How many administrators have seen teachers delivering whole-group instruction while specific kids within that group were clearly not having their instructional needs met? Further, how many of those classes held two, four, or six unused or rarely used computers in the back of the class, each of which held well-designed, research-proven software that would be appropriate for those students? One can only guess at the answer to that question, but two things are clear. First, unused technology is useless technology, and second, teacher training in technology is the key to effective technology applications for instruction.

> *Unused technology is useless technology, and teacher training in technology is the key to effective technology applications for instruction.*

Of course, in beginning to plan for this change process, the school administrators in conjunction with the PLC might wish to canvas the school for both of these factors—technology expertise or technology programs that may already be in use in the school or district. The following schoolwide technology inventory in Box 5.5 might be of use in that process, and certainly PLC members should feel free to adapt this in any way they wish to meet their needs.

Box 5.5   Schoolwide Technology Survey of Resources

The PLC or administrators may wish to survey school faculty with some general questions on faculty expertise in technology, and the possibility of using that expertise for interfaculty coaching. These general questions should assist.

1. Please put a check by the digital technology or applications you use.

    _____Ning   _____blogging   ____Moodle   ____Twitter

    _____Facebook ____e-mail   _____MySpace   ____text messaging

    _____YouTube ___wikis

(Continued)

(Box 5.5 Continued)

2. Would you be willing to provide some informal training to our faculty or select members of our faculty (in groups of three to five) on how you might use these or other digital technologies for instruction? Please explain.

_____

_____

_____

3. Many technologies exist that are not listed above. Can you suggest instructional technologies or digital media that our school should consider for instructional purposes?

_____

_____

_____

4. Do you use any educational software in your class? Please list it here.

_____

_____

_____

5. Have you ever posted a video online? Have you used that in your teaching?

_____

_____

_____

6. What software would you like to use, if the school can provide a budget for purchase?

_____

_____

_____

7. Have you ever received training in various educational technologies that you could share with the faculty at the school? Please describe that here and list the resources you would need for that (e.g., everyone online, or everyone at a computer).

_____

_____

_____

8. Are there particular goals that you believe our faculty should set for moving our school forward in the use of technology? Please list or describe those here.

_____

_____

_____

Given that technology changes more quickly than most persons can follow, it is usually advisable for a teacher to move into increased use of technology for instruction by adapting one or two technologies at a time. For example, if one or two teachers in the school are using wikis for instruction, having other teachers observe that for one or two periods might be enough to help those teachers see how they might use that instructional approach in their own classroom. Likewise, rather than acquire whiteboards for all classrooms, schools might wish to acquire one whiteboard per department and then let the PLC, working with departmental chairpersons, determine who is more likely to use that technology to greatest advantage. Other whiteboards could be acquired in later years. Thus, while technological develop rushes along at breakneck speed, there is no reason teachers have to do so; for teachers who may be less comfortable with technology, have them acquire one or two and implement those first.

CONCLUSIONS

Keep Your Eyes on the Prize!

As educators, our efforts must always be focused on the growth and development of our students over the long term. Toward that end, our teaching practices must change when research has shown that such change enhances our student's academic, behavioral, or social growth. Our primary goal in making any changes in education must be to change a child's life for the better—to enhance achievement and overall success for our students, not merely to follow some educational fad or "strategy of the moment."

The research reviewed throughout this book has documented that these innovations—RTI, technology, and differentiated instruction—will facilitate learning, and in that sense, we undertake these changes in instruction, ultimately, to help our students succeed. Further, given this dynamic synthesis of these factors, if instruction in our classes has not changed drastically within the last three to five years, we may rest assured that we are not offering our students the best instructional practices today. While the concept of differentiated instruction is now a decade old, both RTI and many of the technologies described in this book, while proven by research, are much more recent. For that reason, we simply must update our instructional practices to offer these innovations to our students.

Throughout this text, we have attempted to show how these three catalysts for change—RTI, differentiation, and technology—have created new instructional options for our students, and to state the premise again, the whole is greater than the sum of the parts. Each of these innovations is individually important, but each also feeds from the others and is enriched by a teacher's broad knowledge of the other innovations. We have endeavored to show the excitement and the energy of this three-catalyst interface, this dynamic synthesis, in today's classrooms to demonstrate how technology, RTI, and differentiation can and should work together to benefit all students. The interaction of these three instructional innovations has improved and will continue to drastically improve instruction for our students, and in that sense, today's teachers are in a better position than ever before to assist all students in learning.

> We have endeavored to show the excitement and the energy of this three catalyst interface in instruction throughout this book—to demonstrate how technology, RTI, and differentiation can and should work together to benefit all students.

In conclusion, we strongly recommend these tactics for every educator as the future of instruction in the modern classroom. This is what education for our students can and should be in the early decades of the 21st century, and ultimately, all educators will agree that we owe our students no less than the absolute best instruction that we can provide. This is both our calling as teachers and our obligation to the students and families that we serve.

References

Abernathy, S. (2008). *Responsiveness to instruction: An overview. A presentation on RTI.* Retrieved September 9, 2008, from http://www.ncpublicschools.org/docs/ec/development/learning/responsiveness/rtimaterials/problem-solving/rtioverview-training-present.ppt

Adams, D. M., & Hamm, M. (1994). *New designs for teaching and learning.* San Francisco: Jossey-Bass.

Ardoin, S. P., Witt, J. C., Connell, J. E., & Koenig, J. L. (2005). Application of a three-tiered response to intervention model for instructional planning, decision making, and the identification of children in need of services. *Journal of Psychoeducational Assessment, 23,* 362–380.

Artiles, A. J., Kozelski, E. B., Trent, S. C., Osher, D., & Ortiz, A. (2010). Justifying and explaining disproportionality, 1968–2008: A critique of underlying views of culture. *Exceptional Children, 76*(3), 279–300.

Ash, K. (2010, March 18). Learning benefits seen in laptop initiative. *Education Week, 29*(26), 12–15.

Baker, F. W. (2008). Media literacy: 21st century literacy skills. In H. H. Jacobs (Ed.), *Curriculum 21: Essential education for a changing world* (pp. 133–152). Alexandria, VA: Association for Supervision and Curriculum Development.

Bender, W. N. (2008). *Differentiating instruction for students with learning disabilities: Best teaching practices for general and special educators* (2nd ed.). Thousand Oaks, CA: Corwin.

Bender, W. N. (2009a). *Beyond the RTI pyramid: Solutions for the first years of implementation.* Bloomington, IN: Solution Tree Press.

Bender, W. N. (2009b). *Differentiating math instruction* (2nd ed.). Thousand Oaks, CA: Corwin.

Bender, W. N., & Crane, D. (2010). *RTI in math: Practical guidelines for elementary teachers.* Bloomington, IN: Solution Tree Press.

Bender, W. N., & Larkin, M. J. (2009). *Reading strategies for elementary students with learning difficulties: Strategies for RTI* (2nd ed.). Thousand Oaks, CA: Corwin.

Bender, W. N., & Shores, C. (2007). *Response to intervention: A practical guide for every teacher.* Thousand Oaks, CA: Corwin.

Bender, W. N., & Waller, L. (2011). *RTI and differentiated reading in the K–8 classroom.* Bloomington, IN: Solution Tree Press.

Berkeley, S., Bender, W. N., Peaster, L. G., & Saunders, L. (2009). Implementation of responsiveness to intervention: A snapshot of progress. *Journal of Learning Disabilities, 42*(1), 85–95.

Boyer, L. (2008, June 20). *The West Virginia model for RTI: An update.* Paper presented at the annual Sopris West Educational Conference, Morgantown, WV.

Bradley, R., Danielson, L., & Doolittle, J. (2007). Responsiveness to intervention: 1997–2007. *Teaching Exceptional Children, 39*(5), 8–12.

Bryant, D. P., Bryant, B. R., Gersten, R. M., Scammacca, N. N., Funk, C., Winter, A., et al. (2008). The effects of tier 2 intervention on the mathematics performance of first-grade students who are at risk for mathematics difficulties. *Learning Disability Quarterly, 31*(2), 47–64.

Buffum, A., Mattos, M., & Weber, C. (2009). *Pyramid response to intervention: RTI, professional learning communities, and how to respond when kids don't learn.* Bloomington, IN: Solution Tree Press.

Busch, A. (2010, March 7). Jackson schools using federal stimulus funds to improve reading. *Southeast Missourian.* Retrieved March 20, 2011, from http://www.semissourian.com/story/1616504.html

Caine, R. N., & Caine, G. (2006). The way we learn. *Educational Leadership, 64*(1), 50–54.

Chapman, C., & King, R. (2005). *Differentiated assessment strategies: One tool doesn't fit all.* Thousand Oaks, CA: Corwin.

Chavez, S. (2007, November 5). Grand Prairie Schools welcome iPods in classrooms. *The Dallas Morning News.* Retrieved September 10, 2010, from http://www.dallasnews.com/sharedcontent/dws/dn/education/stories/110507dnmetgpipods.2f9eabc.html

Clarke, K. (2010, January 15). Can school reform ever really work? *U.S. News and World Report,* pp. 25–31.

Cole, J. E., & Wasburn-Moses, L. H. (2010). Going beyond "The Math Wars": A special educator's guide to understanding and assisting with inquiry-based teaching in mathematics. *Teaching Exceptional Children, 42*(4), 14–21.

Cole, S. (2009, June 4). 25 ways to teach with Twitter. *Tech&Learning.* Retrieved September 11, 2010, from http://www.techlearning.com/article/20896

Concept to Classroom. (2004). *What are the essential parts of a WebQuest?* Retrieved September 9, 2010, from http://www.thirteen.org/edonline/concept2class/webquests/index_sub3.html

Connor, D. J., & Lagares, C. (2007). Facing high stakes in high school: 25 successful strategies from an inclusive social studies classroom. *Teaching Exceptional Children, 40*(2), 18–27.

Cooperative learning: Small group learning page. (1997, November 1). Retrieved November 21, 2010, from http://www.wcer.wisc.edu/archive/cl1/CL/default.asp

Cote, D. (2007). Problem-based learning software for students with disabilities. *Intervention in School and Clinic, 43*(1), 29–37.

Davis, M. R. (2010a, March 17). Solving algebra on smartphones. *Education Week, 29*(26), 20–23.

Davis, M. R. (2010b, May 4). District strategies for e-learning. *Education Week.* Retrieved May 7, 2010, from http://www.edweek.org/ew/events/chats/2010/05/04/index.html#info

de Bono, E. (2009). *CoRT 1: Breadth thinking tools: The complete learning, planning, and teaching guide for teachers, administrators, and home schoolers* (CoRT Thinking Lessons). Retrieved from http://debonoforschools.com/pdfs/80850_CoRT1_Introduction_Section.pdf

Denton, C. A., Fletcher, D. D., Anthony, J. L., & Francis, D. J. (2006). An evaluation of intensive intervention for students with persistent reading difficulties. *Journal of Learning Disabilities, 39*(5), 447–466.

Deshler, D. (2010). Interview with the RTI Network. Retrieved February 25, 2010, from www.rti4success.org/index.php?option=com_content&task=view&id=1441

Doidge, N. (2007). *The brain that changes itself.* New York: Penguin Books.

Donovan, M. S., & Cross, C. T. (2002). *Minority students in special education and gifted education.* Washington, DC: National Academy Press.

Drake, K., & Long D. (2009). Rebecca's in the dark: A comparative study of problem-based learning and direct instruction/experiential learning in two 4th grade classrooms. *Journal of Elementary Science Education, 21*(1), 1–16.

Dretzin, R. (Producer/Director). (2011, February 8). *Frontline: Digital nation* [Television broadcast]. New York and Washington, DC: Public Broadcasting Service. Retrieved February 8, 2011, from http://www.pbs.org/wgbh/pages/frontline/digitalnation/

Duffy, H. (2007). *Meeting the needs of significantly struggling learners in high school: A look at approaches to tiered interventions.* National High School Center. Retrieved January 25, 2010, from http://ow.ly/YXW6

DuFour, R., DuFour, R., & Eaker, R. (2008). *Revisiting professional learning communities at work: New insights for improving schools.* Bloomington, IN: Solution Tree Press.

DuFour, R., DuFour, R., Eaker, R., & Karhanek, G. (2004). *Whatever it takes: How professional learning communities respond when kids don't learn.* Bloomington, IN: Solution Tree Press.

DuFour, R., DuFour, R., Eaker, R., & Many, T. (2006). *Learning by doing: A handbook for professional learning communities at work.* Bloomington, IN: Solution Tree Press.

East, B. (2006). *Myths about response to intervention implementation.* Retrieved November 21, 2008, from www.Rtinetwork.org/learn/what/at/MythsAboutRTI

Elder-Hinshaw, R., Manset-Williamson, G., Nelson, J. M., & Dunn, M. W. (2006). Engaging older students with reading disabilities: Multimedia inquiry projects supported by reading assistive technology. *Teaching Exceptional Children, 39*(1), 6–11.

Ferriter, W. M., & Garry, A. (2010). *Teaching the iGeneration: 5 easy ways to introduce essential skills with web 2.0 tools.* Bloomington, IN: Solution Tree Press.

Fleischner, J., & Manheimer, M. (1997). Mathematics interventions for students with learning disabilities: Myths and realities. *School Psychology Review, 26*(3), 397–414.

Fuchs, D., & Deshler, D. D. (2007). What we need to know about responsiveness to intervention (and shouldn't be afraid to ask). *Learning Disabilities Research and Practice, 22*(2), 129–136.

Fuchs, D., Fuchs, L. S., & Stecker, P. M. (2010). The "blurring" of special education in a new continuum of general education placements and services. *Exceptional Children, 76*(3), 301–323.

Fuchs, D., Fuchs, L. S., Thompson, A., Svenson, E., Loulee, Y., Otaiba, S. A., et al. (2001). Peer-assisted learning strategies in reading: Extensions for kindergarten, first grade, and high school. *Remedial and Special Education, 22*(1), 15–21.

Fuchs, L. S., & Fuchs, D. (2007). A model for implementing responsiveness to intervention. *Teaching Exceptional Children, 39*(5), 14–20.

Fuchs, L. S., Fuchs, D., & Hollenbeck, K. N. (2007). Extending responsiveness to intervention to mathematics at first and third grades. *Learning Disabilities Research and Practice, 22*(1), 13–24.

Fuchs, L. S., Fuchs, D., Powell, S. R., Seethaler, P. M., Cirino, P. T., & Fletcher, J. M. (2008). Intensive intervention for students with mathematics disabilities: Seven principles of effective practice. *Learning Disability Quarterly, 31*(2), 79–92.

Gardner, H. (1983). *Frames of mind.* New York: Basic Books.

Gardner, H. (2006). *Multiple intelligences: New horizons.* New York: Basic Books.

Gartner, A., & Riessman, F. (1993, August). Peer-tutoring: Toward a new model. *ERIC Digest.* Retrieved November 2010 from http://www.ericdigests.org/1994/peer.htm (ED362506)

Geisick, K., Graving-Reyes, P., & DeRuvo, S. (2008, May). RtI in a secondary schools setting: Riverbank High School story. Webinar presentation. Retrieved June 2010 from http://www.schoolsmovingup.net/events/rtisecondary

Ghosh, P. (2010). Project based learning. *Buzzle.com.* Retrieved October 9, 2010, from http://www.buzzle.com/articles/problem-based-learning.html

Gibbs, D. P. (2009). *RTI in middle and high school: Strategies and structures for literacy success.* Horsham, PA: LRP Publications.

Gijbels, D., Dochy, F., Van den Bossche, P., & Segers, M. (2005). Effects of problem-based learning: A meta-analysis from the angle of assessment. *Review of Educational Research, 75*(1), 27–61.

Grant, M. M. (2002). Getting a grip on project-based learning: Theory, cases and recommendations. *Meridian, 5*(1). Retrieved October 26, 2010, from http://www.ncsu.edu/meridian/win2002/514/

Greenwood, C. R., Delquadri, J. C., & Carta, J. J. (1997). *Together we can: Classwide peer tutoring to improve basic academic skills.* Longmont, CO: Sopris West.

Greenwood, C. R., Delquardi, J. C., & Hall, R. V. (1989). Longitudinal effects of classwide peer tutoring. *Journal of Educational Psychology, 81*(3), 371–383.

Gregory, G. H. (2008). *Differentiated instructional strategies in practice.* Thousand Oaks, CA: Corwin.

Gregory, G. H., & Kuzmich, L. (2005). *Differentiated literacy strategies for student growth and achievement in grades 7–12.* Thousand Oaks, CA: Corwin.

Gross, S., & Spurka, E. (2010, March 18). *Powering up mobile learning.* Retrieved September 9, 2010, from https://event.on24.com/eventRegistration/Event LobbyServlet?target=registration.jsp&eventid=210162&sessionid=1&key=92C1208822A7F70C9F8F86C32C04EC15

Grossman, L. (2011). 2045: The year man becomes immortal. *Time Magazine, 177*(7), 42–49.

Harper, G. G., & Maheady, L. (2007). Peer-mediated teaching and students with learning disabilities. *Intervention in School and Clinic, 43*(2), 101–107.

Harper, G. G., Maheady, L., Mallett, B., & Sacca, M. (1992). *Classwide student tutoring teams: Instructor's manual.* Fredonia: State University of New York at Fredonia.

Hoover, J. J., Baca, L., Wexler-Love, E., & Saenz, L. (2008). *National implementation of response to intervention (RTI): Research summary.* Retrieved April 2, 2009, from www.nasdse.org/portals/0/national-implementation-or-RTI-Research-Summary.pdf

Hoover, J. J., & Love, E. (2011). Supporting school-based response to intervention: A practitioner's model. *Teaching Exceptional Children, 43*(3), 40–49.

Hoover, J. J., & Patton, J. R. (2008). The role of special educators in a multitiered instructional system. *Intervention in School and Clinic, 43*(4), 195–202.

Hosp, J. (2010). *Ask the expert.* Published by RTI 4 Success. Retrieved July 29, 2010, from http://www.rti4success.org/index.php?option=com_content&task=view&id=1545

Hughes, C., & Dexter, D. D. (2008). *Field studies of RTI programs.* Retrieved November 20, 2008, from http://www.rtinetwork.org/learn/research/field-studies-rti-programs

Jacobs, H. H. (2010). Upgrading the curriculum: 21st century assessment types and skills. In H. H. Jacobs (Ed.), *Curriculum 21: Essential education for a changing world* (pp. 18–29). Bloomington, IN: Solution Tree Press.

James, D. (2010). RTI initiative designed to ID and help struggling students. *Journal Gazette, Times Courier.* Retrieved January 26, 2010, from http://www/jg-tc.com/articles/2010/1/24/news/doc4b5d167ed7de7919688382.txt

Johnson, D. W., & Johnson, R. T. (1999). Theory into practice. *College of Education: Ohio University, 38*(2). Retrieved May 2010 from http://www.fed.cuhk.edu.hk/staff/paper/mmchiu/EDU3310/JohnsonJohnson%20-%20Make%20CL%20work.pdf

Johnson, D. W., Johnson, R. T., & Smith, K. A. (1991). *Cooperative learning: Increasing college faculty instruction productivity* (ASHE-ERIC Higher Education Report No. 4). Washington, DC: George Washington University.

Johnson, D. W., Johnson, R. T., & Smith, K. A. (2007). The state of cooperative learning in postsecondary and professional settings. *Educational Psychology Review, 19*, 15–29.

Johnson, E. S., & Smith, L. (2008). Implementation of response to intervention at middle school: Challenges and potential benefits. *Teaching Exceptional Children, 40*(3), 46–52.

Kame'enui, E. J. (2007). A new paradigm: Responsiveness to intervention. *Teaching Exceptional Children, 39*(5), 6–7.

Kamps, D., Barbetta, P., Leonard, B., & Delquardi, J. (1994). Classwide peer tutoring: An integration strategy to improve reading skills and promote peer interactions among students with autism and general education peers. *Journal of Applied Behavior Analysis, 27*(1). Retrieved September 28, 2010, from http://www.ncbi.nlm.nih.gov/pmc/articles/PMC1297776/pdf/jaba00007-0051.pdf

Katz, L. A., Stone, C. A., Carlisle, J. F., Corey, D. L., & Zeng, J. (2008). Initial progress of children identified with disabilities in Michigan's Reading First schools. *Exceptional Children, 74*(2), 235–256.

Kay, K. (2010). 21st century skills: Why they matter, what they are, and how we get there. In J. Bellanca & R. Brandt (Eds.), *21st century skills: Rethinking how students learn* (pp. xii–xxxi). Bloomington, IN: Solution Tree Press.

King, K., & Gurian, M. (2006). Teaching to the minds of boys. *Educational Leadership, 64*(1), 56–61.

Knowlton, D. (2003). Preparing students for enhanced living. In D. Knowlton & D. Sharp (Eds.), *Problem-based learning for the information age* (pp. 182–199). San Francisco: Jossey-Bass.

Kroeger, S. D., & Kouche, B. (2006). Using peer-assisted learning strategies in increase response to intervention in middle school math settings. *Teaching Exceptional Children, 38*(5), 6–13.

Land, S. M., & Green, B. A. (2000). Project-based learning with the world wide web: A qualitative study of resource integration. *Educational Technology Research and Development, 48*(1), 45–67.

Lange, A. A., Mulhern, G., & Wylie, J. (2009). Proofreading using an assistive software homophone tool. *Journal of Learning Disabilities, 42*(4), 322–335.

Lee, S., Wehmeyer, M. L., Soukup, J. H., & Palmer, S. B. (2010). Impact of curriculum modifications on access to the general education curriculum for students with disabilities. *Exceptional Children, 76*(2), 213–233.

Legere, E. J., & Conca, L. M. (2010). Response to intervention by a child with a severe reading disability: A case study. *Teaching Exceptional Children, 43*(1), 32–41.

Linan-Thompson, S., Vaughn, S., Prater, K., & Cirino, P. T. (2006). The response to intervention of English language learners at risk for reading problems. *Journal of Learning Disabilities, 39*(5), 390–398.

List, J. S., & Bryant, B. (2010). Integrating interactive online content at an early college high school: An exploration of Moodle, Ning, and Twitter. *Meridian Middle School Computer Technologies Journal, 12*(1). Retrieved November 5, 2010, from http://www.ncsu.edu/meridian/winter2009/

Lolich, E., Stover, G., Barker, N., Jolley, M., VanKleek, L., & Kendall, S. (2010). *Response to intervention: Helping all students succeed* [Video file]. Retrieved March 3, 2010, from http://www.rtinetwork.org/Professional/Virtualvisits

Lovett, M. W., De Palma, M., Frijters, J., Steinbach, K., Temple, M., Benson, N., et al. (2008). Interventions for reading difficulties: A comparison of response to intervention by ELL and EFL struggling readers. *Journal of Learning Disabilities, 41*(4), 333–352.

Mahdavi, J. N., & Beebe-Frankenberger, M. E. (2009). Pioneering RTI systems that work! Social validity, collaboration, and context. *Teaching Exceptional Children, 42*(2), 64–72.

Mann, D., Skakeshaft, C., Becker, J., & Kottkamp, R. (1998). *West Virginia story: Achievement gains from a statewide comprehensive instruction technology program.* Santa Monica, CA: Milken Exchange on Education Technology.

Manzo, K. K. (2010a, March 17). Educators embrace iPods for learning. *Education Week, 29*(26), 16–17.

Manzo, K. K. (2010b, March 18). Mobile learning seen to lack rigorous research. *Education Week, 29*(26), 34–36.

Martyn, M. (2007). Clickers in the classroom: An active learning approach. *EdUCause Quarterly, 30.* Retrieved September 10, 2010, from http://www.educause.edu/EDUCAUSE+Quarterly/EDUCAUSEQuarterlyMagazineVolum/ClickersintheClassroomAnActive/157458

Marzano, R. J. (2007). *The art and science of teaching: A comprehension framework for effective instruction.* Alexandria, VA: Association for Supervision and Curriculum Development.

Marzano, R. J. (2010a). *Formative assessment and standards based grading: Classroom strategies that work.* Bloomington, IN: Solution Tree Press.

Marzano, R. J. (2010b). Representing knowledge nonlinguistically. *Educational Leadership, 67*(8), 84–87.

Marzano, R. J., Pickering, D. J., & Pollock, J. E. (2001). *Classroom instruction that works: Research-based strategies for increasing student achievement.* Alexandria, VA: Association for Supervision and Curriculum Development.

McCoy, L. P. (1996). Computer based mathematics learning. *Journal of Research on Computing in Education, 28*(4), 438–460.

McDuffie, K. A., Mastropieri, M. A., & Scruggs, T. E. (2009). Differential effects of peer tutoring in co-taught and non-co-taught classes: Results for content learning and student–teacher interaction. *Exceptional Children, 75*(4), 493–510.

Merzenich, M. M. (2001). Cortical plasticity contributing to childhood development. In J. L. McClelland & R. S. Siegler (Eds.), *Mechanisms of cognitive development: Behavioral and neural perspectives* (p. 68). Mahwah, NJ: Lawrence Erlbaum Associates.

Merzenich, M. M., Tallal, P., Peterson, B., Miller, S., & Jenkins, W. M. (1999). Some neurological principles relevant to the origins of—and the cortical plasticity-based remediation of—developmental language impairments. In J. Grafman & Y. Christen (Eds.), *Neuronal plasticity: Building a bridge from the laboratory to the clinic* (pp. 167–187). Berlin: Springer-Verlag.

Moran, S., Kornhaber, M., & Gardner, H. (2006). Orchestrating multiple intelligences. *Educational Leadership, 64*(1), 23–27.

National Tutoring Association. (n.d.). *National tutoring association: Peer tutoring fact sheet.* Retrieved November 2010 from http://crossroadsoflearning.com/nta-tutorpalooza/pdf/NTA_Peer_Tutoring_Factsheet_020107.pdf

Ojalvo, H., & Schulten, K. (2010, July 9). Tech tips for teachers: Free, easy, and useful creation tools. *Teaching and Learning with the New York Times.* Retrieved September 12, 2010, from http://learning.blogs.nytimes.com/2010/07/09/tech-tips-for-teachers-free-easy-and-useful-creation-tools/?nl=learning&emc=a1

Orosco, M. J., & Klingner, J. (2010). One school's implementation of RTI with English language learners: "Referring into RTI." *Journal of Learning Disabilities, 43*(3), 269–288.

Partnership for 21st Century Skills. (2004). *Framework for 21st century learning.* Retrieved September 9, 2010, from http://www.p21.org/index.php?option=com_content&task=view&id=254&Itemid=120

Partnership for 21st Century Skills. (2007). *21st century curriculum and instruction.* Retrieved November 18, 2009, from www.21stcenturyskills.org/documents/21st_century_skills_curriculum_and_instruction.pdf

Partnership for 21st Century Skills. (2009a). *21st century curriculum and instruction.* Retrieved November 18, 2009, from www.21stcenturyskills.org

Partnership for 21st Century Skills. (2009b). *21st century learning environments.* Retrieved November 18, 2009 from www.21stcenturyskills.org/documents/1e_white_paper-1.pdf

Partnership for 21st Century Skills. (2009c). *The mile guide: Milestones for improving learning and education.* Retrieved November 18, 2009, from www.21stcenturyskills.org/documents/MILE_Guide_091101.pdf

Protheroe, N. (2010). Response to intervention in secondary schools. *Principals' Research Review, 5*(2), 1–7.

Rapp, D. (2009, January). Lift the cell phone ban. *Scholastic Administr@tor.* Retrieved September 12, 2010, from http://www2.scholastic.com/browse/article.jsp?id=3751073

Rhem, J. (1998). Project based learning: An introduction. *National Teaching and Learning Forum, 8*(1). Retrieved October 2, 2010, from http://www.ntlf.com/html/pi/9812/pbl_1.htm

Richardson, W. (2010). *Blogs, wikis, podcasts, and other powerful tools for educators.* Thousand Oaks, CA: Corwin.

Rinaldi, C., & Samson, J. (2008). English language learners and response to intervention. *Teaching Exceptional Children, 40*(5), 6–15.

Rozalski, M. E. (2010). Response to intervention: A rural high school's attempt to improve reading achievement. *CEC Today.* Retrieved January 25, 2010, from http://www.cec.sped.org?AM/Template.cfm?Section=Response_to_Intervention&CONTENDID=11752&TEMPLATE=/CM/ContentDisplay.cfm

Rule, A., & Barrera, M. (2008). *Three authentic curriculum-integration approaches to bird adaptations that incorporate technology and thinking skills.* Informally published manuscript, University of Northern Iowa, Metropolitan State University, Cedar Falls, Minneapolis, MN. Retrieved June 2010 from http://www.eric.ed.gov/PDFS/ED501247.pdf

Salend, S. J. (2009). Technology-based classroom assessments: Alternatives to testing. *Exceptional Children, 41*(6), 48–59.

Silver, H., & Perini, M. (2010). Responding to the research: Harver Silver and Matthew Perini address learning styles. *Education Update, 52*(5), 3–5.

Simmons, D. C., Coyne, M. D., Kwok, O., McDanagh, S., Harn, B. A., & Kame'enui, E. J. (2008). Indexing response to intervention: A longitudinal study of reading risk from kindergarten through third grade. *Journal of Learning Disabilities, 41*(2), 158–173.

Simos, P. G., Fletcher, J. M., Sarkari, S., Billingsley-Marshall, R., Denton, C. A., & Papanicolaou, A. C. (2007). Intensive instruction affects brain magnetic activity associated with oral word reading in children with persistent reading disabilities. *Journal of Learning Disabilities, 40*(1), 37–48.

Smutny, J. F., & Von Fremd, S. E. (2010). *Differentiating for the young child: Teaching strategies across the content areas, PreK–3.* Thousand Oaks, CA: Corwin.

Sousa, D. A. (2005). *How the brain learns to read.* Thousand Oaks, CA: Corwin.

Sousa, D. A. (2009). *How the brain influences behavior.* Thousand Oaks, CA: Corwin.

Sousa, D. A. (2010). *Mind, brain, and education.* Bloomington, IN: Solution Tree Press.

Spectrum K–12. (2009, April). *Response to intervention (RTI) adoption survey 2009.* Washington, DC: Spectrum K–12 School Solutions.

Steedly, K., Dragoo, K., Arefeh, S., & Luke, S. (2008). Effective mathematics instruction. *Evidence for Education, 3*(1). Retrieved July 2009 from http://www.nichcy.org/Research/EvidenceForEducation/Documents/NICHCY_EE_Math.pdf

Sternberg, R. J. (2006). Recognizing neglected strengths. *Educational Leadership, 64*(1), 30–35.

Stevens, R. J., & Slavin, R. E. (1995). The cooperative elementary school: Effects on students' achievement, attitudes, and social relations. *American Educational Research Journal, 32*(2), 321–351.

Stewart, R. M., Benner, G. J., Martella, R. C., & Martella, N. E. M. (2007). Three-tier models of reading and behavior: A research review. *Journal of Positive Behavior Interventions, 9*(4), 239–253.

Strange, E. (2010). Digital history review: The portable past. *American Heritage, 60*(1), 66–68.

Strobel, J., & van Barneveld, A. (2009, Spring). When is PBL more effective? A meta-synthesis of meta-analyses comparing PBL to conventional classrooms. *Interdisciplinary Journal of Problem-based Learning, 3*(1), 44–58.

Tate, M. L. (2005). *Reading and language arts worksheets don't grow dendrites.* Thousand Oaks, CA: Corwin.

Tomlinson, C. A. (1999). *The differentiated classroom: Responding to the needs of all learners.* Alexandria, VA: Association for Supervision and Curriculum Development.

Tomlinson, C. A. (2001). *How to differentiate instruction in mixed-ability classrooms* (2nd ed.). Alexandria, VA: Association for Supervision and Curriculum Development.

Tomlinson, C. A. (2010). Differentiating instruction in response to academically diverse student populations. In R. Marzano (Ed.), *On excellence in teaching* (pp. 247–270). Bloomington, IN: Solution Tree Press.

Tomlinson, C. A., Brimijoin, K., & Narvaez, L. (2008). *The differentiated school: Making revolution changes in teaching and learning.* Alexandria, VA: Association for Supervision and Curriculum Development.

Tomlinson, C. A., & McTighe, J. (2006). *Integrating differentiated instruction and understanding by design: Connecting content and kids.* Alexandria, VA: Association for Supervision and Curriculum Development.

Topping, K., & Elhy, S. (Eds.). (1998). *Peer assisted learning.* Mahwah, NJ: Erlbaum.

Torgesen, J. K. (2007, June). *Using an RTI model to guide early reading instruction: Effects on identification rates for students with learning disabilities.* Florida Center for Reading Research. Retrieved December 12, 2008, from www.fcrr.org

Tsay, M., & Brady, M. (2010). A case study of cooperative learning and communication in pedagogy: Does working in teams make a difference? *Journal of the Scholarship of Teaching and Learning, 10*(2). Retrieved July 2010 from http://www.eric.ed.gov/PDFS/EJ890724.pdf

Vaughn, S., Wanzek, J., Murray, C. S., Scammacca, N., Linan-Thompson, S., & Woodruss, A. L. (2009). Response to early reading intervention: Examining higher and lower responders. *Exceptional Children, 75*(2), 165–183.

Wachanga, S., & Mwangi, J. (2004). Effects of the cooperative class experiment teaching method on secondary school students' chemistry achievement in Kenya's Nakuru district. *International Education Journal, 5*(1). Retrieved June 2009 from http://ehlt.flinders.edu.au/education/iej/articles/v5n1/wachanga/paper.pdf

What Works Clearinghouse. (2010, September). *Intervention: Classwide peer tutoring.* U.S. Department of Education Institute of Education Sciences. Retrieved October 3, 2010, from http://ies.ed.gov/ncee/wwc/reports/english_lang/cwpt/index

Wilmarth, S. (2010). Five socio-technology trends that change everything in teaching and learning. In H. H. Jacobs (Ed.), *Curriculum 21: Essential education for a changing world* (pp. 80–96). Alexandria, VA: Association for Supervision and Curriculum Development.

Wood, C. L., Mackiewicz, S. M., Norman, R. K., & Cooke, N. L. (2007). Tutoring with technology. *Intervention in School and Clinic, 43*(2), 108–115.

Index

CORWIN
A SAGE Company

The Corwin logo—a raven striding across an open book—represents the union of courage and learning. Corwin is committed to improving education for all learners by publishing books and other professional development resources for those serving the field of PreK–12 education. By providing practical, hands-on materials, Corwin continues to carry out the promise of its motto: **"Helping Educators Do Their Work Better."**